HEDGES

*Creating screens
and edges*

HEDGES

Creating screens and edges

AVERIL BEDRICH

GUILD OF MASTER CRAFTSMAN PUBLICATIONS

First published 2001 by
Guild of Master Craftsman Publications Ltd,
166 High Street, Lewes,
East Sussex, BN7 1XU

ISBN 1 86108 216 9
A catalogue record of this book is available from the British Library

All photographs supplied by Harry Smith Horticultural Photographic Collection except:
David Bradford, pp 124, 125, and caterpillars on p 126
George Culpan, honey fungus on p 126
Eric Sawford, p 61

Black-and-white illustrations by John Yates
Colour illustrations by Melanie Clitheroe

Designed by Fran Rawlinson
Cover design by Danny McBride
Typefaces: Garamond, Helvetica Neue

Colour origination by Viscan Graphics (Singapore)
Printed and bound by Kyodo Printing (Singapore) under the supervision of MRM Graphics,
Winslow, Buckinghamshire, UK

To Gerry for a shared love of gardening and to
Natasha, Emma and Mark for spending so much time gardening
while they were growing up.

Contents

Introduction

When my husband and I set up a business selling hedging plants, it became clear that there was very little in the way of information relating to the use and growth of hedges. Perhaps this is because hedges are taken so much for granted or because, with the grubbing up of so many country hedges since the 1950s, no-one got round to writing much about them.

Many of our clients had numerous questions about their choice of plants, and about siting and planting, pruning and maintenance. We certainly sold a large number of hedging plants and their diversity was fascinating. So many of the shrubs were well known but somehow, when used for hedging, clients felt a little mystified as to their cultivation. I hope this book will allay any fears or misgivings about using such a range of plants for hedging and will encourage readers to replace existing man-made borders with living boundaries – an ecological improvement for our environment.

As I hope you will discover, the planting and care of hedges is not a complicated affair, except perhaps for the more unusual forms such as topiary, pleaching or plashing. Hedges can be very uncomplicated and beautiful boundaries, personalizing our own living spaces.

LEFT *Berberis julianae*

THE HEDGE

*Evolution and
Environment*

History

BARRIERS AND PROTECTION

Since the days of Neolithic man (4500–2000BC), hedges have been used to provide stockproof barriers and to mark out boundaries. When forests were first cleared to provide an area in which to keep domestic animals, boundaries were formed to protect it. These would have had three uses:

- to confine and prevent the animals escaping;
- to protect them from attack by predators; and
- to stake out a claim on territory.

The Romans recorded the use of hedges as a means of protection as far back as 55BC when they encountered plashed, or layed, hedges in Flanders used as defences against their invasion. Even further back Alexander the Great (356–323BC) had come up against the same problem when he invaded Persia. Plashed hedging is still used to mark farm boundaries, though the art is now less common than it once was. I have seen hawthorn hedges plashed in early spring and they looked wonderful as their buds swelled and burst into leaf and flower.

Plashing requires the annual pruning of a hedge. It involves cutting the branches, bending them horizontally, and weaving them together. This encourages new shoots to grow vertically from the breaks in the old branches, to produce new, dense growth in the spring. The impenetrable hedge this produces makes a very effective stock barrier.

LEFT *Myrtus communis* (common myrtle)

DECORATION

Elaborate treatments can be traced back to the Romans; they preferred living boundaries to man-made alternatives because they lasted longer and were less costly to maintain. Their love of tall hedges and enjoyment of gardens led them to use hedges for recreation and relaxation. Alcoves and seating areas were created within them either to display sculpture or provide spaces for sitting and resting.

Basic clipping of evergreen hedges developed into topiary, with box, rosemary, cypress and holm oaks all being shaped. Yew did not feature much in Britain until the late seventeenth century, due to its sacred associations; very large yews were believed to be over 2,000 years old and therefore, to have been in existence since before Christ. It was not until the more enlightened period of the Restoration that yew became much sought-after for use in hedging and topiary.

LEGENDS

Many traditional hedging shrubs and trees have a history of associated legend and superstition. In Greek mythology, myrtle was dedicated to Venus, the goddess of love, and brides carried sprigs of it in their bouquets as a symbol of loyalty and love. The hawthorn was an emblem of hope for the ancient Greeks and was dedicated to the goddess Persephone. The Romans later adopted this emblem, dedicating it to their goddess Flora.

Holly has many religious associations, some dating back to medieval times, when monks called it the Holy Tree. Its links with Christmas are reflected in its old names 'prickly Christmas' and 'Christ's thorn'. According to British folklore, elves and fairies join in the Christmas celebrations if they are allowed to hide in the holly's branches. In return for this, they protect the inhabitants from the mischief of the house goblin. The ancient Greeks

Corn circle, of unknown origin, enclosed by an indigenous hedge

thought that a holly bush planted near a house would protect it from lightning and keep away evil spirits. Witches are said to hate holly because of its prickles, and its red berries are said to ward off evil as red is a magically potent colour.

REGIONAL CHARACTERISTICS

Hedges in early Anglo-Saxon times (AD 410–1066) were often 'dead', made from sticks and twigs, brushwood and woven willow wands, but these were replaced by 'quick' hedges as it was found that sticks from some of the very prickly shrubs – such as blackthorn (sloe) and hawthorn (quick) – soon rooted and grew when stuck in the ground. Blackthorn and hawthorn have since become the most widely used plants for quickset hedges and nearly always make up the bulk of an indigenous mixed hedge.

In Anglo-Saxon times, however, hedges were regional, existing in some areas but not others. In the ninth century quick hedges were found predominantly in woodland areas and this regional tradition did not alter radically until the enclosure acts of the twelfth century came into force.

A fine example of a wild, native hedge

AGRICULTURAL DEVELOPMENT

The Anglo-Saxons were the first to put a pattern on the landscape by clearing forests and woodlands and forming hedges around their settlements when they began agriculture as we know it. Where dead hedges or protective wattle boundaries had been erected and later abandoned, 'living' hedges would form from the seedlings dispersed by wildlife. Birds perched on top of dead hedges would drop or excrete the seeds of brambles, rosehips, elderberries and hawthorn, amongst others, which they had carried from neighbouring woodlands.

The traditional English rural scene, of fields forming a patchwork across the land, was created by the planting of hedgerows. The enforcement of the Parliamentary enclosure acts added to this quilt over many years. A number of enclosure acts were passed over the centuries, many between the twelfth and fourteenth centuries, with the final acts passed between the eighteenth and nineteenth centuries. One of the earlier enclosure movements, which affected the Midlands and Northumberland, occurred during the period between 1460 and 1600. Acts continued up until 1903. Because of these England, and southern England in particular, became crisscrossed by little lanes between fields. Some fields were softened by rounded corners which made it easier for a horse and plough to turn in bygone days and for a tractor to turn today.

Most countryside hedgerows and hedges were planted with just one or two woody species but gradually, with wind blowing in seeds from other shrubs and trees and birds dispersing seeds in their travels, the traditional mixed hedgerow has come into existence. The successful germination and growth of different species is dependent on soil conditions, among other things, so indigenous hedges evolved, with those in different regions being composed of different species. In south-west the individual areas. Hedgerow trees are referred to in Anglo-Saxon records, from AD 410 to 1066, indicating that hedgerows at this time would have included rows of standard trees, such as holly, oaks, hornbeam and hawthorn, along their line.

FARMING

Hedges have had many uses in farming. In areas like the Weald of Kent, where the soil is very heavy clay, hedges were planted with ditches dug alongside to drain off surplus water. This practice dates back to Roman times and is still in use today. Such hedges also provide a natural environment for wildlife and shade for smaller farm animals, such as sheep, who often shelter in their lee in hot weather.

As farming became more intensive and large, unimpeded areas of land were required, hedgerows were grubbed up. Hedges fell into decline in the latter part of the eighteenth century and many were grubbed up as a result of the enclosure acts and agricultural subsidies of the time. Later, between 1951 and 1980, large numbers of hedges were grubbed up as a consequence of the financial incentives offered to farmers to encourage more intensive farming. This has had a very detrimental effect on soil conditions as winds then blew straight across the surface of the land, stripping it of the topsoil. Hedges act as a buffer and a windbreak, and gaps in them help to regulate frosty air by allowing it to seep through in small amounts; without these gaps, pockets build up until they rise and flow over the hedge in one large mass, which severely damages crops. The planting of particularly high hedges, often in excess of 6ft (1.8m), is still practised in fruit-growing areas to help reduce the damage that late frosts can cause to blossoms. Hedges, because of their need for water, reduce surface run-off and the risk of flooding, and this in turn reduces soil erosion, thus enabling farmers to utilize their fields for different crops.

Dating hedgerows

It is fascinating that just by looking at the botanic richness of the area surrounding old hedgerows it is possible to get an idea of their age. An abundance of bluebells and wood anemones, which are slow colonizers, suggests that the area has been left untouched since medieval times, when the original woodlands were cleared, so the old hedgerows could well date back to that period also. To date a hedgerow, count the number of species present in its length: each of these equates to 100 years, so if you count four different species, the hedge is probably 400 years old.

Ireland, for instance, fields and roads are often lined with fuchsia hedges while neat, thick hawthorn hedges are still common in the Midlands, and in Staffordshire, hedges are often composed largely of holly. In the Somerset Levels hedges of osier rise around the flood areas whilst in Kent and Hereford and Worcester, where there are hop and fruit farms, hedges are often high and densely planted to shelter the fruit from frost. This difference reflects the native shrubs and plants that are easy to grow in

Ecology and wildlife

LIVING BOUNDARIES

In the twenty-first century much emphasis is being placed on ecological and environmental issues and we are all greatly aware of the need to preserve our natural surroundings. Those of us who are keen gardeners or who need to enclose our gardens can help by planting 'living' boundaries or windbreaks instead of erecting man-made fences. Not only do hedges look softer, their value to wildlife and native flora is immense.

COUNTRYSIDE

Shelter and protection

A hedge is a haven for wildlife and imperative to its preservation. Hedges in the countryside, and in particular those nearest existing woodland areas, make the largest contribution to the survival of native birds and mammals.

Firstly, hedges provide safe corridors or lanes through which small mammals can move from one area to another without having to venture into the open, where they could become the target of predators. It is important to note that hedges surrounding large areas of arable land, where woodlands are either non-existent or have been grubbed out, do not create the same environment and corridors as those nearer original woodlands.

LEFT Large Skipper butterfly on bramble

A blackbird's nest safely nestled in the foliage of a hedgerow

Thrushes enjoying the protection of a holly hedge

Secondly, hedgerows, particularly mixed, thorny, quickset ones, make ideal nesting habitats for birds – many species rely on them for their procreation. In late spring, when hawthorns are bursting into life, nesting is at its peak. The hawthorn provides much shelter in its leafy boughs and dense twiggy growth. Often an indigenous hedge, which usually consists of at least 45% hawthorn, is the only suitable cover for woodland nesting birds. This is particularly so in intensively farmed areas but less important in more wooded regions. Pairs of robins, hedge sparrows, great tits, blackbirds, wrens and bluetits all need woodland or hedgerows for their nests to provide protection from other, larger predatory birds such as jackdaws and crows.

Thirdly, many useful insects, including butterflies and bees, hover around hedgerow plants. Hedgerow butterflies lay their eggs on the stalks of cuckooflower and hedge garlic so that as their larvae develop, they can feed on the flora throughout the summer. The larvae then pupate in the autumn and remain in the hedgerows, dormant, throughout the winter.

Food

Besides providing safe habitats for insects, birds and mammals, hedgerows act as host to many wild flowers. Climbers, such as the wild old man's beard and the wild honeysuckle, weave their way through the branches, attaching themselves by way of tendrils, or prickles in the case of bramble, providing birds, mammals and human beings alike with fruits. The wild hop, wild dog roses, common ivy and bindweed all enjoy this natural environment.

In the spring and summer months the natural flora of the countryside comes into its own and a great variety of wild flowers flourish in the hedgerows, enabling the natural cycle of the wildlife that depends upon them to continue.

The ground beneath hedges supports primroses, cow parsley, wild strawberries, sweet violets, periwinkle, dandelions, burdock, common foxgloves, great willowherb, vetches, and goosegrass to name but a few.

Comfrey, cow parsley, herb Robert, wood anemones, lords-and-ladies (also known as cuckoopint), red campion, vetch, stitchwort and the great assortment of natural grasses would soon diminish without the sturdy presence of our hedgerows. These, in their turn, produce pollen for bees and fruits, nuts and berries for birds.

Peacock butterfly on buddleja

The many different plant species growing in and under country hedges can be a great source of food for wildlife through spring, summer, autumn and winter

To coppice simply means to cut a woody plant down to the ground. This encourages new shoots to grow from its base. It is widely practised in woodland areas in order to maximize the wood that can be harvested. As it is carried out every two or three years, the light level in woodland areas alters regularly, with the change either stimulating or slowing down the rate of growth of herbaceous plants endemic to the area. For instance, bluebells, wood anemones, primroses and ferns, which are shade tolerant, burst into life if a layer of woodland is removed, allowing warmth and light to reach the earth beneath. Biennial plants such as foxgloves, or the more short-lived perennials like the red campion, find space among the cleared woodland floor only to be forced out to the margins again when young saplings begin to invade the space.

This method of husbandry can be transposed to our gardens where, in large plots, coppiced shrubs can create environmentally friendly, informal edges to the plot and, at the same time, provide food and shelter for plant- and wildlife. If the nut- and berry-producing species of shrubs, such as corylus (hazelnut) and sambucus (elder) are used, their autumn fruits add to the country store cupboard for our birds and small mammals.

In winter the same hedgerows provide food for birds and woodland animals: berries and nuts from the hedging plants themselves, seed heads from the many species which grow naturally amongst them, and seeds from the many native grasses.

COPPICING

Although a coppice is not hedging in the strict sense of the word, it is a form of screening or shelter belt and, as several traditional hedging plants are also commonly coppiced, contributing greatly to the wellbeing of wildlife and countryside flora, it is worth inclusion here.

These bluebells have sprung up as a result of woodland clearance

A low-growing hedge of cotoneaster 'decorating' footpath and steps in a landscaped town garden

TOWN AND VILLAGE

Shelter and protection

Town and village gardens can extend the ecological benefits provided by hedging. Evergreen hedges of laurel, holly, and rhododendron are perfect winter habitats for roosting birds such as finches, starlings, yellowhammers, thrushes and blackbirds, whilst a thick hawthorn hedge, like the quickset country hedge, offers a protective habitat for the nests of smaller birds. Tall hedges can also provide shelter for greenfinches and house sparrows.

Food

The fragrant, flowering hedges and windbreaks often used in cultivated gardens are a regular source of winter food for birds and small mammals. There are berries from cotoneasters and filberts from *Corylus avellana,* with its catkins appearing in spring. Pyracantha, *Chaenomeles japonica* and the Berberidaceae family, which are often planted to produce deterrent or protective hedges, are all flush with bright berries in the autumn; as well as being attractive, these provide another source of regular winter fare.

UNDERPLANTING

Underplanting with hardy perennials will place a screen or hedge in a more cultivated setting, but is still an environmentally friendly option. Hardy perennials such as hardy geraniums, *Viola odorata,* and *Brunnera macrophylla* will soon colonize the area, adding flowers and foliage from spring through to summer. Dogwood has lovely bright stems which provide colour and interest in the winter. It needs to be cut back really hard, almost coppiced in fact, to achieve the new, brilliantly coloured growth.

DIRECTORY

*Choosing
the right plants*

Traditional hedgerows

TRADITIONAL, INDIGENOUS MIXES

A traditional, indigenous mix for planting your own hedgerow is as follows, including the number of plants required for each species:

Crataegus monogyna (common hawthorn) 15
Prunus spinosa (blackthorn) 10
Acer campestre (field maple) 5
Viburnum opulus (guelder rose) 3
Viburnum lantana (wayfaring tree) 2
Rosa canina (dog rose) 5

These 40 plants would produce a 10yd (9m), semi-staggered row with four plants per yard (metre). It is best to buy hedging plants bare-root, between late autumn and early spring, when they can be planted out. Many nurseries now specialize in bare-root hedging plants and trees and it is by far the cheapest and easiest way of both buying and planting an indigenous hedge. *Crataegus monogyna* and *Prunus spinosa* traditionally make up 40–50% of the mix as they knit the hedge together; the other plants can be interwoven along the run. This gives the hedge a lovely countryside appearance and also leaf, berry and flowering interest throughout the year.

LEFT *Crataegus monogyna* (common hawthorn)

TRADITIONAL HEDGEROWS

Acer campestre

Carpinus betulus

Cornus alba see p 34

Corylus avellana see p 54

Crataegus monogyna

Euonymus europaeus see p 79

Fagus sylvatica

Ilex aquifolium see p 29

Prunus spinosa

Rosa canina

Rosa multiflora

Rosa pimpinellifolia

Rosa rubiginosa (syn. *R. eglanteria*) see p 66

Viburnum lantana

Viburnum opulus

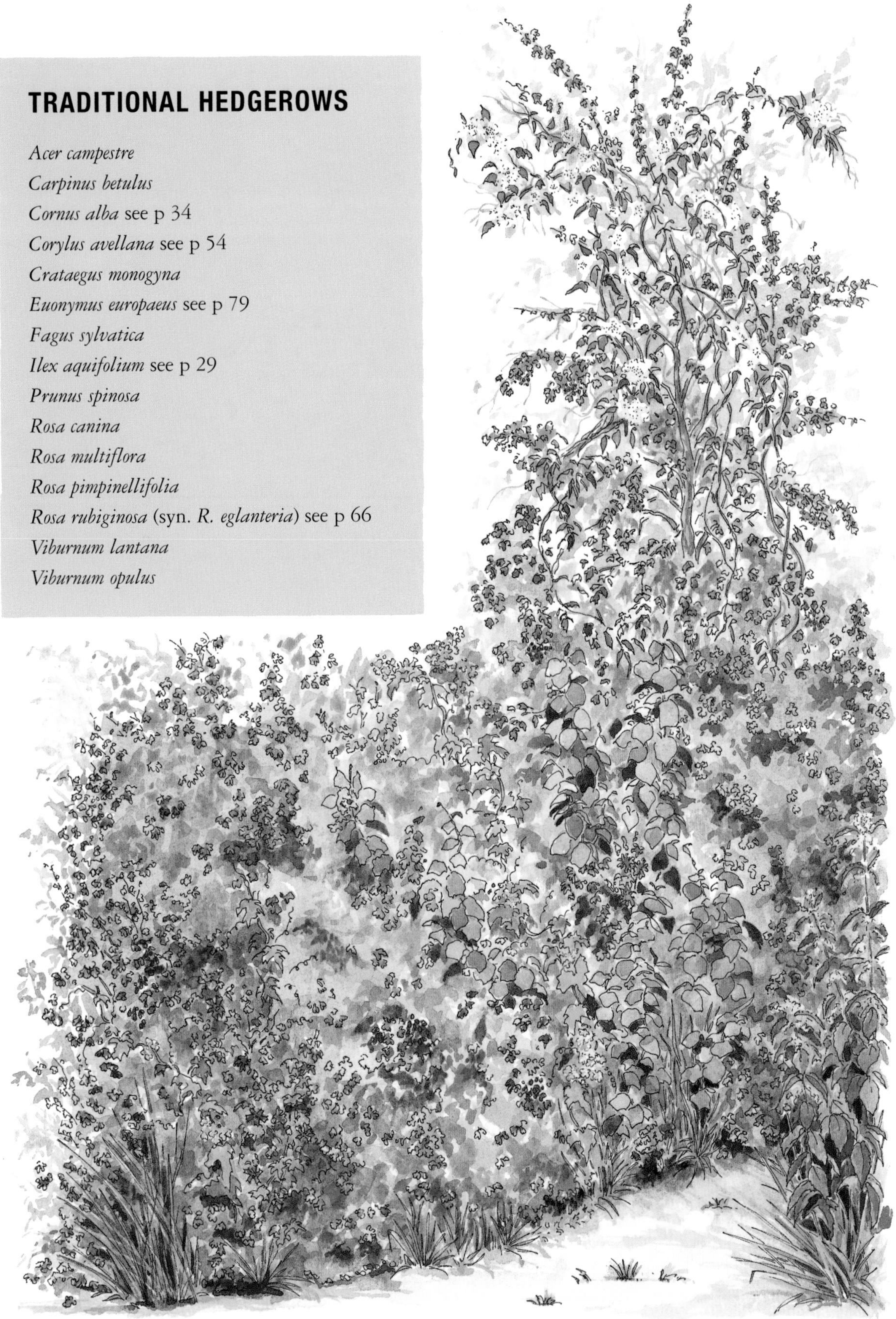

Carpinus avellana

TRADITIONAL HEDGEROWS

Acer campestre (field maple, hedge maple)

Also called field or hedge maple, this is a medium-sized tree with foliage that turns clear yellow, sometimes flushed with red, in autumn. It is often used in rustic country hedges, is fast growing and likes any well-drained soil. For hedges of 4–15ft (1.2–4.5m), plant 18in (45cm) apart. In a mixed hedge, plant along the run to your preference.

Carpinus betulus (common hornbeam)

This deciduous tree can be trimmed into the most glorious of hedges. The oval, ridged, dark green leaves turn to rich oranges and yellows in the autumn. From late spring to autumn green catkins are produced and in late autumn these turn into clusters of winged nuts, providing winter food for

wildlife. *Carpinus betulus* will grow in any well-drained, fertile soil, in sun or partial shade. It lends itself well to the traditional country hedge and to more formal, cultivated garden boundaries.

Crataegus monogyna (common hawthorn)

Also known as common hawthorn, this shrub is the most common in hedgerows and is very distinctive. It has dark, glossy green leaves and an abundance of white, fragrant flowers in spring, followed by red fruits or haws in autumn. It is fast growing and tolerant of wet soils. For hedges of 3–20ft (1–6m), plant 9–12in (22–30cm) apart. For denser hedges, plant in a staggered, double row with 15in (35cm) between the rows and 18in (45cm) between the plants. In a mixed hedge, follow the above planting distances but plant in groups of three or five along the run to form the backbone of the hedge.

Fagus sylvatica (common beech)

This much-loved hedging plant is one of the most popular choices for both country and town hedges. It likes any well-drained soil in sun or shade and is fully hardy. Its wavy, dark green leaves change to the most wonderful golden hue in autumn, and the dying leaves are held on the interwoven branches throughout the winter. *Fagus sylvatica* can be clipped into formal shapes when required or mixed with other plants in an indigenous hedge for a less formal appearance.

Prunus spinosa (blackthorn, sloe)

Also known as sloe and blackthorn, this is a very thickly growing shrub or small tree with dark, spiny branches which are covered in tiny, star-like flowers in early spring. Fruits, or sloes, follow in autumn. These are like small damsons and appear with a blue bloom before becoming a shiny black. Sloes can be used for preserves, in wine making and for flavouring gin. The branches provide traditional blackthorn sticks and Irish shillalahs (stout clubs or cudgels). For hedges of 3–10ft (1–3m), plant 18in (45cm) apart. For a mixed hedge, plant as for *Crataegus monogyna* (see above), to form the backbone of the hedge. Trim with hedging shears whenever necessary.

Rosa canina (dog rose)

This is the familiar hedge rose. It is a large, rambling shrub with very strong, prickly stems. The fragrant flowers are white or pink, about 1½–2in (4–5cm) in diameter, and are followed by large, red, egg-shaped hips in autumn. *Rosa canina* is often used to thicken a mixed hedge, so plant wherever necessary or to your liking. Prune by trimming with shears or secateurs, depending on the thickness of the branches.

Rosa multiflora

This is one of the fragrant, white, rambling roses that are often used to scramble through indigenous hedges. It is extremely vigorous, has pea-like fruits in winter, adding to the store of food for wildlife, and is ideal for thickening hedges or covering ugly banks. This rose is described more fully in the section on roses (see p 69).

Rosa pimpinellifolia (syn. R. spinosissima) (Scotch rose, burnet rose)

This rose, often known as the scotch or burnet rose, has a dense, suckering habit which lends itself admirably to hedging. Its fern-like, light green leaves and prickly stems make it a beautiful but impenetrable barrier and its sweetly scented lemon flowers and shiny black fruits add interest from spring to autumn. This rose is described more fully in the section on roses (see p 66).

Rosa pimpinellifolia 'Dunwich Rose'

Viburnum lantana (wayfaring tree)

This large shrub is a familiar sight in hedgerows. It is particularly happy on chalk, so grows well on the Downs in southern England. The creamy-white, rather insignificant flowers are followed by rich red fruits which turn black in the autumn; this is also the time when the leaves – broad, ovate and hairy on their underside – turn a dark crimson. Plant individually wherever needed and prune with secateurs or shears, depending on the thickness of the stems.

Viburnum opulus (guelder rose)

This viburnum, the guelder rose, is also known as the water elder. It is a large, vigorous shrub with maple-like leaves which give glorious autumn colour. In early and midsummer, the large, flat flowerheads resemble the flowers of the elder. These are followed in autumn by shiny red fruits which last well into the winter months. *Viburnum opulus* particularly likes moist, boggy areas, as its common name suggests. It is frequently used in hedges and woodland areas. Plant individually wherever needed and prune as for *V. lantana* (see left).

FARM BOUNDARIES

Hedgerows have long been associated with farming – over the last two centuries. In many areas of Britain, particularly regions like East Anglia, the move to arable farming on a large scale necessitated the grubbing up of many old hedgerows. However, where they are still in use, one of the main priorities for the farmer is that they be stockproof. It is important to remember, therefore, that some hedging plants are poisonous to livestock. The plants listed in the panel on p 19 are poisonous to animals if eaten in any quantity so

Viburnum lantana (wayfaring tree)

it is essential not to use these plants anywhere near where animals can reach whilst grazing.

Hawthorn and hornbeam are often firm favourites for stockproof barriers on farms, as both are extremely sturdy and grow very thick. Hawthorn has the added advantage of thorns, which knit the hedge tightly together, and is also more tolerant of wet conditions than hornbeam. However, hornbeam tends to be more tolerant of cold, exposed positions. Both plants can be maintained by mechanical hedge cutters, so their care is uncomplicated for the farmer.

Where tall hedges are planted as windbreaks for orchards, care must be taken to provide filter areas at their base so that frost pockets, which can build up behind them, can pass through. Cold air is denser than warm and drops to the bottom of a valley or slope, so a hedge can be an effective barrier. However, cold air fills up the cavity behind the hedge and will eventually spill over the top, thus damaging crops or blossoms growing behind it. Small gaps should be left at regular intervals

Warning

These plants are poisonous to livestock

box	laurel
broom	rhododendron
cypress	yew

along the hedgerow by pruning back the trunks of the plants. These allow the cold air to filter through, causing considerably less damage than otherwise. The same applies to all boundary hedges that are protecting crops or plants. Remember, hot air rises and cold air descends.

Indigenous hedgerows still exist in smaller farms and are particularly suitable for country boundaries. In our more ecologically and environmentally aware world today there is much interest in planting indigenous hedges once again.

Specific conditions

SEASIDE AND COASTAL SITES

In my research on hedges I have been amazed at how many plants are tolerant of littoral positions. One of the beauties of planting in a coastal area is that there is less danger of frost and the air is much cleaner than inland. Humidity levels are higher on the coast and some areas also benefit from warm sea currents; it is these conditions which allow the more tender plants to survive. However, salty and buffeting winds can be as damaging as cold, frosty weather – salt spray can burn leaves as if they have been exposed to flames. Some plants are more resistant to these conditions and it is important to differentiate between exposed cliff edges and high watermark areas, which only certain hedging shrubs can stand, and the more sheltered positions inland where quite tender plants will often happily survive.

ABOVE *Euonymus japonicus*
LEFT *Kalmia latifolia*

SEASIDE AND COASTAL SITES
Exposed gardens

Atriplex halimus
Brachyglottis (Dunedin Group) 'Sunshine'
Buddleja davidii
Elaeagnus x *ebbingei*
Escallonia rubra var. *macrantha*
Euonymus japonicus
Genista hispanica

Hippophae rhamnoides
Juniperus spp.
Laurus nobilis
Olearia x *haastii*
Olearia macrodonta
Prunus spinosa

Pseudosasa japonica
Quercus ilex
Sambucus nigra 'Aurea'
Spartium junceum
Tamarix spp.
Ulex europaeus

Exposed gardens

Atriplex halimus (tree purslane)

This plant is particularly valuable for its silvery grey leaves – its small green flowers are quite insignificant. It makes an informal, loose hedge that is able to withstand any amount of salty sea spray and wind.

Atriplex halimus will reach 6–8ft (15–20cm) on poorer, but well-drained soils but does not like to be waterlogged.

Brachyglottis (Dunedin Group) 'Sunshine'

Formerly known as *Senecio* 'Sunshine', this plant has tough grey foliage and a profusion of yellow, daisy-like flowers in large, open panicles. It forms a loose, shaggy hedge and adds brightness to a screen or boundary. Being sun-loving and wind-resistant, it is particularly suitable for coastal conditions. To keep it in shape, it is best pruned after flowering.

Buddleja davidii

A popular flowering shrub and useful for screening. This is described in more detail in the section on flowers and fragrance. (See p 48.)

Elaeagnus x ebbingei

In late summer this evergreen shrub has white, scented, bell-shaped flowers borne above dark green, oval leaves with a silvery underside. It can reach 15ft (4.5m) in height and needs clipping to keep it thick and in shape. It is a particularly good windbreak as it has a high tolerance of sunshine and windy sea spray.

Escallonia rubra var. macrantha

This is a very popular choice for seaside gardens because it will withstand wind and sea spray. However, it performs best in the milder coastal areas where its glossy, dark green leaves set off the masses of crimson-red flowers from early summer

Genista hispanica (Spanish gorse)

to mid-autumn. Being evergreen, it will give a good hedge throughout the year. It is a vigorous grower and will reach up to 10ft (3m) but can be trimmed to whatever height is required.

Euonymus japonicus (Japanese spindle)

This is a strong-growing evergreen plant. While not noted for any particularly interesting features, it does make a good hedge in coastal areas. It has large, oval, glossy green leaves with small green flowers appearing in spring, sometimes followed by pink fruits in autumn. Suitable for either sun or shady areas. *Euonymus japonicus* 'Macrophyllus Albus' is a variegated form of this dense, bushy shrub, with large oval leaves edged in white.

Genista hispanica (Spanish gorse)

This deciduous, spiny shrub grows to about 3ft (1m), and has a mass of bright yellow, pea-like flowers in early summer. It likes a well-drained, sandy soil in sun and is very wind tolerant.

Hippophae rhamnoides (sea buckthorn)

This thorny plant loves the windy, salty conditions of the coast. It has slender, silvery, willow-like leaves followed, in autumn, by masses of orange-yellow berries which stay on the branches throughout winter. It is fast growing and likes well-drained soil. It can be trimmed into shape in late summer.

Juniperus spp. (juniper)

Junipers will tolerate a very heavy, salt-laden position so are ideal for planting in exposed areas, but they do need a well-drained, sunny site to thrive. They tend to be used to add architectural interest to a garden or, as specimen trees, to add colour.

Laurus nobilis (bay laurel)

This will form a dense formal hedge if regularly clipped. The aromatic leaves are a favourite flavouring for meat dishes such as daubes or stews

Hippophae rhamnoides (sea buckthorn)

and for stocks, soups and curries. It thrives in coastal areas but will suffer frost damage if exposed to intense cold, so a milder climate is preferred.

Olearia x haastii

This dense, bushy, evergreen shrub, native to New Zealand, is ideal in milder coastal districts. Its felty green leaves, grey underneath, show off pretty white, slightly perfumed, daisy-like flowers. These are followed by fluffy seed heads in autumn. Pruning in spring will keep it neat and tidy. It also enjoys a sunny position with well-drained soil.

Olearia macrodonta

Olearia macrodonta is a very robust species with lovely, large flower heads.

Prunus spinosa (blackthorn)

This is particularly good for the outer edges of a very exposed site. *Prunus spinosa* (see photo on p 24) is described in more detail in the section on traditional hedgerows. (See p 17.)

Pseudosasa japonica

Pseudosasa japonica is a very hardy species of bamboo which grows well in the British Isles. Strictly speaking, these shrubs do not form traditional hedges but loose, waving screens which are particularly attractive near water and are ideal for screening a pond or lake. Its olive green canes form dense clumps. If planted near water the sunlight filters through the canes, throwing dappled light onto the surface of the pond or lake. The vigorous and invasive root system of *P. japonica* is especially useful at the water's edge as the interwoven roots help hold the banks together. Its broad, evergreen leaves form a shelter or shield around the water in much the same way as an evergreen hedge would around a garden.

Quercus ilex (holm oak)

This is a magnificent tree with its ridged bark and leathery, glossy green leaves, but clipped hard it will form a stiff, wind-resistant hedge in coastal areas, where it thrives. It is particularly beautiful in early summer when its new white shoots and yellow catkins are unfurling.

Prunus spinosa (blackthorn)

Sambucus nigra 'Aurea' (golden elder)

This fast-growing shrub has large clusters of creamy-white flowers in early summer, followed by large bunches of black elderberries in autumn; these make delicious wine. The beauty of this sambucus is its glorious golden colour during spring and summer; when growing in shade this brightens the surrounding area. It needs to be cut back very hard in spring in order to restrict its growth. It is ideal for large areas and as a windbreak.

Spartium junceum (Spanish broom)

This deciduous plant has almost leafless branches. Its bright yellow, fragrant, pea-shaped flowers appear from early summer right through to autumn. Spanish broom is very wind-resistant and enjoys an exposed, sunny position.

Tamarix spp.

These graceful deciduous shrubs make good informal hedges and windbreaks. Their feathery, softly coloured foliage adds a Mediterranean feel to a garden, particularly on the coast. They have a tendency to become top-heavy, so do need cutting back hard on a regular basis to encourage growth from the base. There are three main species suitable for hedges and windbreaks, all of which need fairly well-cultivated soil to flower well.

Tamarix gallica

Tamarix gallica has star-shaped, pink flowers which form slender racemes in late spring and early summer.

Tamarix ramosissima

Formerly known as *T. pentandra*, this species has bluish-green leaves and upright plumes of pink flowers from midsummer to early autumn.

Tamarix tetrandra

Tamarix tetrandra has reddish-pink flowers in late spring and requires pruning back after flowering.

Ulex europaeus (gorse)

This is a vigorous shrub whose dense, dark green shoots and vicious spines give it the appearance of being evergreen. It has fragrant, pea-like yellow flowers from early to late spring. It will thrive in poor, dry, acid soils but is also suitable for any well-drained soil in sun. When grown as a hedge it can be trimmed after flowering to maintain a compact habit.

SEASIDE AND COASTAL SITES
Sheltered gardens

Corokia x *virgata*
Escallonia cvs
Fuchsia spp.
Fuchsia magellanica
Griselinia spp.
Griselinia littoralis
Griselinia lucida
Hebe spp.
Hebe x *franciscana* 'Blue Gem'
Hebe rakaiensis
Hydrangea macrophylla
Pistacia lentiscus
Pittosporum tobira

Sheltered gardens

Away from the salty sea spray and sheltered from the worst of the winds, almost any hedge is possible. In the warmer coastal areas in particular, some of the more tender or half-hardy shrubs will survive.

Corokia x virgata

This medium-sized, evergreen shrub, native to New Zealand, makes an interesting hedge in milder coastal areas. It has an erect habit with oblong, tapering, green-grey foliage. Although evergreen, it can defoliate if the weather is particularly cold. The tiny, starry yellow flowers are usually followed by bright orange fruits.

Escallonia cvs

This genus is particularly suited to the coastal garden. It has no fussy soil requirements but does need full sun. It responds well to clipping and flowers continuously from early summer to mid-autumn. Varieties with an arching habit make a wonderful loose, informal, flowering hedge.

In addition to the *Escallonia rubra* var. *macrantha* mentioned in the hardier section above (see p 22), the following cultivars can be used for hedges:

E. 'Apple Blossom', has apple-blossom pink flowers and a dense and bushy habit

E. 'Donard Seedling' has pale pink flowers and an arching habit

E. 'Iveyi', with pure white, fragrant flowers, is more upright in habit

E. 'Langleyensis' has rose pink flowers and an arching habit

Fuchsia spp.

The showy *Fuchsia* 'Mrs Popple', with its vigorous, arching branches of red-and-purple, tubular flowers, can make a glorious informal hedge in a more sheltered garden.

Fuchsia magellanica

The most popular species for hedging is *Fuchsia magellanica*. This deciduous shrub has beautiful, pendulous, red-and-purple flowers followed by purple fruits. It can grow to about 6ft (1.8m). *Fuchsia m.* 'Riccartonii' is a hardier cultivar with its young red wood and is particularly attractive.

Griselinia spp.

Native to New Zealand, these prefer warm regions.

Fuchsia 'Mrs Popple'

Griselinia littoralis

Griselinia littoralis is a dense, evergreen, upright shrub which can make a large hedge. To restrict growth, it must be trimmed in early summer. It enjoys a sunny, well-drained position. The oval leaves are pale green and yellowish-green flowers appear in late spring. *Griselinia littoralis* 'Dixon's Cream' is slower growing, and has creamy markings in the centre of the leaf.

Griselinia lucida

Griselinia lucida, even faster growing than *G. littoralis*, has shiny, dark green leaves.

Hebe spp.

This genus of evergreen shrub is another favourite for coastal regions as it thrives in sea air as long as it is in a well-drained, sunny position. It is most suitable for a smaller hedge and can be cut back in spring to restrict its growth. *Hebe* 'Autumn Glory' forms a mound of reddish-purple shoots, round, dark green leaves and deep purple flowers from early summer to mid-autumn.

Hebe x franciscana 'Blue Gem'

This cultivar is particularly wind-resistant and is ideal around the coast except in the coldest regions. Its oblong, dark green leaves throw into contrast the thick, stubby spikes of violet-blue flowers and give a dense, colourful hedge.

Hebe rakaiensis

Hebe rakaiensis makes a lovely, lower-growing hedge with its tiny white flowers covering the stems in early and midsummer. It is very versatile as it is one of the hardier hebes and can withstand most conditions, although it prefers full sun.

Hydrangea macrophylla

This shrub is more fully described in the section on flowers and fragrance, but it is particularly suitable for coastal areas. (See p 55.)

Pistacia lentiscus

This drought-resistant, grey-green shrub responds well to hard clipping and would make an interesting hedge in a sheltered, sunny area. Its foliage turns varying shades of red in the autumn. Although it originates from the maquis or scrubland of the Mediterranean and is one of that region's colonizing plants, it will tolerate frost and conditions of down to 19.4°F (–7°C).

Pittosporum tobira (Japanese pittosporum, mock orange)

This is the least hardy of all the hedging plants suitable for coastal areas but it does make an excellent evergreen hedge and is drought-resistant. It loves a bright, sunny position. The leathery, glossy leaves set off its fragrant, creamy flowers, which appear in late spring. *Pittosporum tobira* can make a large hedge so to keep in shape, prune judiciously, with secateurs, in late spring when any fear of late frosts is over, but before the flowers appear. For those who want to plant a hedge in warmer climates, this plant is used frequently for hedging in the South of France, where its drought-resistant qualities are invaluable.

Hebe rakaiensis

WINDY SITES

Carpinus betulus

Chamaecyparis lawsoniana

Crataegus monogyna

x *Cupressocyparis leylandii*

Ilex aquifolium cvs

Prunus cerasifera

Prunus cerasifera 'Pissardii'

Prunus laurocerasus

Prunus lusitanica

Pseudosasa japonica

Sambucus nigra

Taxus baccata

WINDY SITES

Many of the hardier seaside shrubs described above
will make good hedges in any part of the country
where wind is a problem as they have to cope with
winds coming off the sea. However, it must be
remembered that in particularly windy locations,
the height of the hedge makes a considerable
difference. Wind is not blocked by a hedge, but
filtered and diverted; as it passes upwards and over
the hedge, it will hit the ground at a different
point. Therefore, it is important to consider the
height of the hedge if you need a lot of wind
protection in your garden. In filtering wind, a
hedge will reduce its strength and turbulence by
about 40%, and it will deflect it by a distance of
approximately ten times its height.

The first garden that we created from scratch was
very exposed and wind whistled across the adjoining
farmland with ferocity. We sometimes felt that there
was little between us and Siberia. In order to protect
our newly designed Elizabethan garden just in front
of the cottage, and to stop the wind from whirling
against the window panes, we planted a hedge of
Prunus laurocerasus (cherry laurel). In the space of
about five years, this grew to over 12ft (6.5m) high
and 3ft (1m) wide. We cut it back to 10ft (3m) and
this afforded us a beautifully protected garden in
spite of the ferocious winds.

In a similar way, fruit orchards are often protected
by high hedges of conifers, often the ubiquitous
x *Cupressocyparis leylandii*, as seen in many areas in
Kent. In Provence, in the South of France, the fruit
orchards are shielded in much the same way. In
Britain these hedges also protect fruit blossom
from late frosts.

Carpinus betulus (common hornbeam)

As part of a mixed native hedge, this makes an
extremely good wind break. *Carpinus betulus* is
described more fully in the section on traditional
hedgerows. (See p 16.)

Chamaecyparis lawsoniana (lawson cypress)

This is a conical evergreen conifer with dark green
foliage and upright branches. It requires very little
clipping and can grow up to 20 x 8ft (6 x 2.5m) in
the space of 20 years. It prefers semi-shade and
moist soil conditions.

Crataegus monogyna (quickthorn)

As with *Carpinus betulus*, this species makes an
excellent windbreak used as part of a mixed native
hedge. *Crataegus monogyna* is described in the
section on traditional indigenous mixes. (See p 16.)

x *Cupressocyparis leylandii*

These grey-green conifers are very fast growing and
enjoy being in a well-drained, sunny position. They
do make very good windbreaks but in smaller
gardens are often too vigorous at the expense of
other plants. A popular species is x *Cupressocyparis
leylandii* 'Galway Gold' (syn. 'Castlewellan') which
is slightly less vigorous. This is grown for its
bronze-gold foliage. (See also p 38.)

Chamaecyparis lawsoniana (lawson cypress)

Ilex aquifolium cvs (common holly)

These evergreens are very dense and prickly with glossy green foliage and red berries in winter. Only the pollinated female of the species produces berries so a male must be planted somewhere nearby. There are a number of cultivars, both green-leaved and variegated, which make good hedges; I have listed some female and male examples below. The

male cultivars are more numerous so I have listed only the species most suitable for hedges.

Female

I. a. 'Alaska' is a green-leaved variety. This prickly, compact shrub produces abundant red berries

I. a. 'Argentea Marginata' has broad leaves edged with cream

I. a. 'Handsworth New Silver' is free berrying, with dark green, cream and grey leaf variegation and purple stems – a very handsome holly indeed

I. a. 'Madame Briot' has purple bark and a variegated leaf

Male

I. a. 'Atlas' has dark green leaves and is very hardy

I. a. 'Ferox' is a hedgehog holly; there are spines over nearly all the leaves, which are slightly variegated and very attractive

I. a. 'Ferox Aurea' is very similar to *I. a.* 'Ferox', described above

Planting different hollies together in a hedge gives a very pleasing effect and also increases the chances of good berrying in the winter. A dark green holly interspersed with one of the variegated varieties can look quite dramatic. In addition to tolerating windy conditions, hollies can tolerate shade, so the variegated species can also be used to brighten up dark areas. Trim in late summer to keep in shape.

Prunus cerasifera (cherry plum)

This is one of the standard hedging plants and makes a dense, strong-growing hedge very quickly. It has tiny white flowers in early spring, sometimes as early as late winter, and can be planted with *Prunus cerasifera* 'Pissardii' to make a very attractive, multicoloured hedge.

Prunus cerasifera 'Pissardii'

This plant is also known as the purple blaze plum because of its purple stems and dark red foliage which changes to deep purple. It has tiny whitish-pink flowers from early to mid-spring and it makes the most attractive dense purple hedge. It will grow in any location and in any soil.

Prunus laurocerasus (cherry laurel)

This evergreen is one of the most regularly used plants for hedging. It provides protection and an air of formality. Its lovely, glossy leaves make a wonderful backdrop for most gardens except, perhaps, the smallest: laurel is a vigorous plant once established. The most important thing to remember when planting a laurel hedge is to keep it well watered at the beginning. Even small plants of 16–24in (40–60cm) will respond quickly if well looked after in their early days. Their energy goes into making a good root system first, so leaf drop on newly planted laurels often occurs. Do not worry. Once the roots are happily established, the hedge will take off.

Prunus cerasifera 'Pissardii'

Many people are put off laurel because it has to be pruned with secateurs and not with a hedge cutter. When growing a large hedge, this is a serious consideration. Initially, I trimmed our laurel hedge with secateurs to encourage the new growth and to keep a good shape, but as it got bigger this posed a problem and we succumbed to the hedge cutters, both manual and electric. It responded beautifully.

The only negative aspect of mechanical clipping is that some of the leaves will be damaged, but once the new growth starts, the damaged leaves fade into the background of the hedge. Laurels should be cut back from late summer to early autumn to allow new growth to harden off before the winter.

Prunus lusitanica (Portugal laurel)

This is very similar to cherry laurel but makes a more compact hedge. The pointed, dark green leaves have red stems and scented, white flowers which appear in early summer, followed by small red fruits which turn black in winter. There is also a variegated form and both make interesting hedges. *Prunus lusitanica* should be treated in the same way as *P. laurocerasus* (see p 45) and cut back in summer or early autumn.

Pseudosasa japonica (bamboo)

This plant is very hardy and wind-resistant and grows particularly well in damp areas. It makes a dense hedge or screen but its roots are invasive so care must be taken when siting. (See p 105.)

Sambucus nigra (common elder)

Sambucus nigra is particularly good in a windy spot and suitable for chalky sites as well. It is deciduous, with attractive, filigreed leaves. The flattened heads of its white flowers, which appear in early summer, can be used in elderberry wine. Elder needs to be pruned hard each spring to keep its growth in check. Hard pruning will also keep the foliage fresh and young.

Prunus lusitanica (Portugal laurel)

Taxus baccata (English yew)

This dense, evergreen shrub has bright red berries which attract birds in winter. It will tolerate any soil and shade and is very hardy.

Taxus baccata make wonderful formal hedges and are well suited to topiary. If planted correctly, they also make fairly fast-growing hedges, contrary to common belief. Dig a deep trench, line this with well-rotted manure, then cover with a layer of earth before planting the young plants. This will encourage the roots to settle deep into the ground as they reach down for nutrients present in the well-rotted manure.

I also added a good handful of bonemeal to each yew when I planted a hedge and from small, 12in (30cm) plants I had a beautiful, thick, 4ft (1.2m) hedge within 3–4 years. Again, keep well watered while very young. Once established, a regular feed of seaweed extract, both in the soil and as a foliar feed, will keep *T. baccata* dark green and healthy.

DRY, SHADY SITES

Buxus sempervirens (see p 41)
Elaeagnus spp. (see pp 42 and 43)
Euonymus fortunei 'Emerald Gaiety'
Euonymus fortunei 'Emerald 'n' Gold'
Hypericum x *moserianum*
Ilex aquifolium (see p 29)
Ligustrum ovalifolium (see p 44)
Prunus laurocerasus (see p 30)
Prunus lusitanica (see p 30)
Ribes alpinum
Symphoricarpos albus var. *laevigatus*

DRY, SHADY SITES

Euonymus fortunei 'Emerald Gaiety'

This evergreen produces variegated leaves, predominately rich green and white which become tinged with pink in autumn.

Euonymus fortunei 'Emerald 'n' Gold'

Another evergreen, the leaves of this cultivar also become flushed with pink in autumn. At other times its green leaves have bright gold margins that lighten to cream.

Hypericum x moserianum

This deciduous, arching shrub bears saucer-shaped, yellow flowers with red anthers from midsummer to early autumn. It thrives in a shady position, where it can make a low-growing, informal hedge, but will tolerate partial shade as well.

Ribes alpinum (alpine currant)

This is a neat, densely twiggy form of the flowering currant. It thrives in poor soil and will tolerate shade. It has mid-green leaves in mid-spring after which it becomes smothered with dainty, greenish-yellow flowers. *Ribes alpinum* can be trimmed after flowering and again in late summer to keep it in shape.

Ribes alpinum (alpine currant)

Symphoricarpos albus var. laevigatus (snowberry)

This strong-growing, deciduous shrub is ideal for providing cover for game birds. On large estates it is often planted specifically for this purpose. As it grows well in poor soil and dark places it can be used for hedges in difficult, shaded areas. Clusters of small white flowers appear from late spring to early summer, followed by glistening white berries in autumn and winter. It has a strong suckering habit so is not suitable for small areas.

DRY, SUNNY SITES

Berberis julianae (see p 53)
Buxus microphylla var. *japonica*
Cistus spp.
Cistus laurifolius
Cistus 'Silver Pink'
Lavandula angustifolia (see p 60)
Myrtus communis
Pittosporum tobira (see p 50)
Rosmarinus officinalis (see p 60)
Santolina chamaecyparissus (see p 60)
Teucrium fruticans (see p 62)

DRY, SUNNY SITES

Buxus microphylla var. japonica

This variety, if left to its own devices, will grow into a small tree, but it responds extremely well to regular clipping and because of this, is frequently used for dwarf hedging and topiary.

Because of its drought-resistant qualities, *B. m.* var. *japonica* is better suited to dry, sunny areas than *B. sempervirens*. It is slow growing but will reach 4 x 4ft (1.5 x 1.5m).

Myrtus communis (common myrtle)

Cistus spp.

Cistus make wonderful flowering hedges for dry, sunny sites. They are very wind-resistant so would suit maritime gardens, but they are not suitable for polluted areas, cold or damp situations as they are true sun lovers, and are susceptible to frost.

Most *Cistus* species grow to around 3ft (1m). They do not respond well to pruning so are fairly short-lived. However, if you have the right conditions, they will reward you with an abundance of flowers, and many have perfumed foliage which is accentuated by the warmth of the sun.

Cistus laurifolius

One of the most popular species for hedging, this has dark green, leathery leaves and pure white flowers with yellow centres. It is one of the hardiest species, and can reach 6½ft (2m).

Cistus 'Silver Pink'

Another hardy and popular species for hedging. As the name suggests, this has silvery pink flowers, which grow in long clusters.

Myrtus communis

Perfect for formal, dense hedging in hot, sunny areas. Hardy in sheltered, inland and seaside sites, it is considered tender in many other areas so take care with its siting. It is evergreen and can be clipped in the same way as buxus. All you need is a sharp pair of hedge clippers or sheep shears. Once the hedge has reached the desired height, clip it into shape and keep the hedge line crisp with regular clipping. Treated in this way it will thicken fairly quickly. *Myrtus communis* has small, aromatic green leaves, and tiny white flowers in spring, followed by blue-black berries in autumn. *Myrtus communis* subsp. *tarentina* is a dwarf variety.

WET SITES IN SUN OR SHADE

Alnus glutinosa
Cornus alba
Cornus sanguinea
Corylus avellana (see p 54)
Crataegus monogyna (see p 16)
Pseudosasa japonica (see p 24)
Viburnum opulus (see p 18)

WET SITES IN SUN OR SHADE

I have grouped sun and shade together in this list as there are only a few hedging plants that need a lot of moisture.

Alnus glutinosa (common alder)

This makes a lovely tall, narrow hedge or screen which loves a wet, boggy site. In spring its elegant catkins are particularly attractive and the screen or hedge which the plant produces has a lovely light, airy appearance.

Cornus alba (red-barked dogwood)

Cornus alba has brilliant red stems which make a bold display in winter. It is best planted in clumps rather than as a traditional hedge in order to maximize the effect of the green leaves, which turn a brilliant orange-red in autumn. Their shape and colour add winter interest, particularly near ponds. To keep the colour of the bark, the plants need to be pruned hard in spring.

Cornus sanguinea

This hedgerow plant can be included in any traditional, indigenous hedge mix where the conditions are right – they like a damp position but are tolerant of chalky soils. The green stems are flushed with red and go on to produce superb autumn colour.

Cornus alba (red-barked dogwood)

LIME-FREE SITES

Erica spp.
Kalmia latifolia
Rhododendron spp.
Rhododendron ponticum
Spiraea douglasii
Tsuga canadensis

LIME-FREE SITES

The following plants are acid loving, so they need lime-free soil to flourish. This is not a large selection. In fact, the only obvious plants which could be used for hedging in lime-free soils are kalmias and rhododendrons for large hedges and ericas and spiraeas (but only one or two species) for lower-growing hedges.

Erica spp. (heather)

These low-growing hedging plants are described in more detail in the section on evergreens. I have also included them here because of their preference for lime-free soils. (See p 41.)

Kalmia latifolia (calico bush, mountain laurel)

This is an evergreen and enjoys the same lime-free conditions as rhododendrons. In early summer, its beautiful clusters of pink flowers are shown off by the surrounding, dark, glossy foliage. Careful pruning with secateurs keeps this shrub in trim and although it makes an attractive informal screen, if pruned, it can attain a degree of formality.

Rhododendron spp.

Rhododendrons are such a large and specialized subject, I will only touch on them lightly. If you want to plant a hedge of rhododendrons, I would recommend that you seek more detailed advice.

There is an amazingly large selection of species which are wonderful to grow but their siting must be given careful consideration.

Rhododendron ponticum

Rhododendron ponticum is among the most common species. It is the most popular choice for creating shelter belts and hedges. Its pink-mauve flowers are almost luminous during late spring and early summer. They need very little maintenance once established as long as they are planted in a suitable position. *Rhododendron ponticum* will grow happily in both dry and damp conditions and tolerates shade. It is very invasive, so site with care.

Spiraea douglasii

This is a very vigorous, suckering shrub with dark, purple-red flowers in early and midsummer. Spiraea varieties tend to be tolerant of most conditions, but this one is acid-loving.

Tsuga canadensis

Tsuga canadensis, a lovely, graceful, arching conifer, loves acid and well-drained soil. It is covered in more detail in the section on evergreens. (See p 40.)

CHALK AND LIMESTONE

Berberis darwinii (see p 52)
Carpinus betulus (see pp 16 and 28)
Chamaecyparis lawsoniana (see p 28)
Cornus sanguinea (see p 34)
x *Cupressocyparis leylandii* (see p 28)
Fagus sylvatica (see p 17)
Ilex aquifolium (see p 29)
Olearia macrodonta (see p 23)
Rugosa roses (see p 72)
Taxus baccata (see p 31)
Thuja plicata (see p 40)
Viburnum tinus (see p 51)

Evergreens

SHAPE AND DEFINITION

An evergreen hedge, cared for and kept well clipped, often gives a garden its vital shape, particularly when it is used to divide large areas into individual 'rooms' or to define walkways (see p 92). Evergreen hedging does not have to be formal and there are many plants, including those listed below, that can be used to screen or protect areas of the garden.

ABOVE *Elaeagnus pungens* 'Maculata'

LEFT *Quercus ilex* (holm oak)

INFORMAL HEDGES

Abelia x *grandiflora* (see p 52)

Atriplex halimus (see p 22)

Berberis x *stenophylla* (see p 53)

Ceanothus spp. (see p 54)

Corokia x *virgata* (see p 25)

Escallonia cvs (see p 26)

Eucalyptus spp. (see p 43)

Euonymus japonicus (see p 23)

Hebe spp. (see p 26)

Hypericum x *moserianum* (see p 32)

Kalmia latifolia (see p 35)

Mahonia aquifolium (see p 48)

Olearia x *haastii* (see p 23)

Osmanthus delavayi (see p 49)

Photinia x *fraseri*

Potentilla fruticosa (see p 57)

Rhododendron spp. (see p 35)

Ulex europaeus (see p 25)

Viburnum tinus (see p 51)

INFORMAL HEDGES

Photinia x *fraseri*

This hardy hybrid evergreen shrub has large, glossy, dark green leaves which are bright red when young. The young growth is particularly resistant to late frosts but holds its colour well into the summer months. It will grow in any fertile, well-drained soil, in sun or partial shade, but does prefer shelter from strong winds. *Photinia* x *fraseri* 'Red Robin' is a particularly colourful cultivar which bears large heads of creamy white flowers in late spring.

CONIFERS AS HEDGES

Chamaecyparis lawsoniana (see p 28)
x *Cupressocyparis leylandii*
x *Cupressocyparis leylandii* 'Galway Gold'
  (syn. *C. l.* 'Castlewellan')
Cupressus macrocarpa
Juniperus virginiana
Taxus baccata
Taxus cuspidata
Taxus x *media* cvs
Thuja plicata 'Atrovirens'
Tsuga canadensis

CONIFERS AS HEDGES

One of the main advantages of using conifers for hedging is that they are evergreen. They will provide a dense, impenetrable hedge and can be clipped into neat, formal shapes.

On the down side, they are greedy eaters and as a consequence, will rob much of the surrounding soil of both moisture and nutrients. However, planted in the correct position, they add symmetry and privacy to a garden.

x *Cupressocyparis leylandii*

This hybrid is very vigorous and fast growing but can be ideal if a tall, protective windbreak is required. The main problem with x *C. leylandii* is the speed at which it grows once established, so careful siting is imperative. If used in smaller gardens (which I would not recommend) they can be overpowering if not kept tightly and regularly clipped. They also starve the surrounding soil thus making it difficult, if not impossible, to grow anything else near them. However, in the right place, they make a very dense boundary. They are often used to form tall hedges in orchards and fruit farms to protect early spring blossoms from wind and frost damage.

x *Cupressocyparis leylandii* 'Galway Gold' (syn. *C. l.* 'Castlewellan')

As its name suggests, this is a golden hybrid, but turns bronze-green with age. This cultivar is slower growing and therefore more suitable for hedging than x *C. leylandii*. 'Galway Gold' was a seedling raised at Castlewellan, in Co. Down, in 1962. It is a cross between the female *Cupressus macrocarpa* 'Lutea' and *Chamaecyparis nootkatensis* 'Lutea'.

Cupressus macrocarpa (Monterey cypress)

A fast-growing conifer. The cultivar 'Lutea' has a soft golden hue which turns green as it ages. It has a compact habit but needs to be trimmed in late summer to maintain its shape. This species is also ideal for coastal regions but the young plants are susceptible to cold so care needs to be taken when choosing a site.

Juniperus virginiana

This is the hardy version of *Juniperus chinensis* (Chinese juniper). Its foliage is fragrant when cut and varies from dark green to silvery bluish-green but in some plants turns to a dark plum in winter. It needs a well-drained, sunny position and will tolerate any dry, sandy or exposed areas.

Cupressus macrocarpa (Monterey cypress)

Juniperus virginiana 'Hillii' makes a good hedge as it is one of the slower-growing cultivars; it will grow to a height of 5–12ft (1.5–3.5m). Juniperus is particularly useful in difficult positions such as salt-laden coastal areas and among urban planting.

Taxus baccata (English yew)

Taxus is an invaluable evergreen in all but the smallest gardens and is tolerant of many different conditions and sites. It has dark leaves with bright red berries which attract birds in winter. It can play a major part in the soft landscaping of garden design as its dense, evergreen foliage is excellent for topiary as well as hedges. This species is described in more detail in the section on windy sites (see p 31).

Taxus cuspidata (Japanese yew)

Taxus cuspidata is slightly hardier than *T. baccata* and is good for particularly cold areas.

Taxus x *media* cvs

Taxus cultivars that are particularly suitable for hedges include *T.* x *media* cultivars. (*Taxus* x *media* is a cross between *T. baccata* and *T. cuspidata*.) The three most useful of these are:

T. x *media* 'Brownii', a columnar male form

T. x *media* 'Hicksii', a columnar female bush

T. x *media* 'Sargentii', a female bush with an erect
and dense growth habit

Thuja plicata 'Atrovirens' (western red cedar)

Thuja plicata makes a large, fast-growing hedge
with glossy, bright green leaves and cinnamon-red,
shredding bark. When crushed, the leaves are
aromatic. It prefers moist but not waterlogged soil
and will tolerate chalk.

Tsuga canadensis (eastern hemlock)

This graceful, gently arching conifer makes a lovely,
tightly knit hedge with small, pendulous cones that
ripen during their first year and remain until the
second. It likes a well-drained, moist, acid soil and
will tolerate full sun or partial shade but does not
like a windy, exposed situation. Clipped regularly,
it can be kept as low as 3ft (1m) but will grow as
high as 50ft (15m)! For a formal hedge, prune each
summer, after the first flush of growth.

FORMAL HEDGES
Small

Berberis buxifolia 'Nana'
Berberis x *stenophylla* 'Irwinii'
Berberis thunbergii f. *atropurpurea*
Buxus spp.
Buxus sempervirens
Erica spp.
Erica x *darleyensis*
Erica vulgaris
Hebe rakaiensis
Hedera helix 'Glymii'
Lonicera nitida cvs
Osmanthus heterophyllus
Sarcococca confusa

FORMAL HEDGES
Small
Berberis buxifolia 'Nana'

A slow-growing, spiny plant with small, rounded
leaves not unlike box. It produces orange flowers
and dark purple fruits and can eventually reach a
height of 3ft (1m). Trimming lightly in spring will
keep it thick and to the required height.

Berberis x *stenophylla* 'Irwinii'

Berberis x stenophylla 'Irwinii'

A small, compact shrub with deep yellow flowers.
It is ideal for dwarf hedges. Trim after flowering.

Berberis thunbergii f. atropurpurea

This form is probably one of the most popular of
the genus with its wonderful rich red-purple
foliage, which becomes bright red in autumn.

Buxus spp.

Buxus like any well-drained soil in a sunny position
– water-logged soils must be avoided. As a large
number of plants are needed to grow a hedge, the
cheapest and easiest way to start one is to buy plants
very small and place them fairly close together;
about 9in (20cm) apart gives a good, dense hedge.
When clipping off the tops initially, take cuttings.

These root fairly easily in a good compost mix of sharp sand, and a little bit of heat from underneath will help them on their way. It is always handy to have a supply of box plants, however small, to use as fill-ins, either for gaps or to replace failures.

Buxus sempervirens (common box)

Buxus sempervirens, as its common name suggests, is the most frequently used species for hedging. It grows naturally into a small tree but is particularly suitable for regular clipping and because of this, is frequently used as dwarf hedging. It has always been one of the most used plants for knot gardens and parterre (formally patterned flower gardens) and for edging potagers (small kitchen gardens combining vegetables and decorative plants). *Buxus sempervirens* 'Variegata', a variegated cultivar, makes a lovely dwarf hedge with an overall golden effect.

Erica spp. (heather)

Ericas make good low hedges on lime-free sandy soil, peat, or rich loamy soil.

Erica x darleyensis

Erica x *darleyensis*, which has pink flowers from late autumn to early spring and grows to about 2ft (60cm), is one of the few heathers that will tolerate a limy soil. In colours from white through to dark crimson, they make a bright, cheerful dwarf hedge right through the autumn into late winter and early spring. Trimming after flowering will keep them in shape.

Erica vulgaris

Along with *Erica* x *darleyensis*, E. *vulgaris* is the most popular species of heather to be used for dwarf hedging. This variety flowers from late autumn to early spring.

Hebe rakaiensis

This hebe makes a lovely low-growing, sturdy, evergreen hedge and has the added bonus of producing masses of tiny white flowers in early and midsummer. It has green-grey leaves which respond well to regular clipping.

Hebe rakaiensis

Hedera helix 'Glymii'

This ivy, although classed as a climber, is particularly suitable for fast-growing but low hedges. In Victorian times, ivies were used for many purposes, in particular for edging paths and display areas. *Hedera helix* 'Glymii' has the added bonus of leaves that turn a brilliant bronze-red in autumn.

Lonicera nitida cvs (poor man's box)

A small-leaved, evergreen shrub which has been used for formal, clipped hedges for many years and can also be used in topiary. It is quick growing and responds well to a pair of shears. *Lonicera nitida* can reach a height of 5–6ft (1.5-1.8m).

Three cultivars which make very good hedges are:

L. n. 'Baggesen's Gold', a golden-leaved form which turns dark in the autumn. New growth is predominantly yellow

L. n. 'Ernest Wilson', the most commonly used for hedging. This has a slightly arching growth and tiny oval leaves

L. n. 'Yunnan', very similar to 'Ernest Wilson' but stouter and more erect.

Osmanthus heterophyllus

This holly-like, slow-growing osmanthus makes a lovely, dense, evergreen hedge. It has dark green, shiny leaves and sweetly perfumed flowers that appear in autumn. Its prickly leaves make it a good subject for deterrent hedges and it can also be used effectively for topiary.

Sarcococca confusa (sweet box)

I have described *Sarcococca confusa*, a lovely shrub, more fully in the section on flowers and fragrance. (See p 61.) However, I feel it must also be included here because of its evergreen properties and low-growing habit.

FORMAL HEDGES
Large

Aucuba japonica
Elaeagnus x *ebbingei* cvs
Elaeagnus pungens 'Maculata'
Eucalyptus gunnii
Griselinia littoralis
Ilex aquifolium
Laurus nobilis
Ligustrum spp.
Ligustrum japonica
Ligustrum ovalifolium
Ligustrum ovalifolium 'Aureum'
Ligustrum vulgare
Prunus spp.
Prunus laurocerasus
Prunus lusitanica
Quercus ilex

Large
Aucuba japonica

This is an evergreen, shade-loving plant which will thrive in almost any condition. There are many cultivars and some of the variegated forms are quite beautiful. One example is *A. japonica* 'Crotonifolia' whose leaves are blotched with gold. They make lovely, dense, shrubby hedges and the variegated plants lighten a dark corner. To keep in shape, pruning is best done with secateurs, in spring.

Elaeagnus x ebbingei cvs

Elaeagnus x *ebbingei* is a very accommodating shrub with several cultivars, all evergreen. They respond well to hard pruning and grow on most soils and in most conditions. They also have tiny, fragrant silver flowers in autumn followed by orange fruits in spring. The following cultivars are suitable for creating relatively formal hedges if clipped, and informal shelter belts if left to their own devices:

E. x *e.* 'Gilt Edge', a cultivar whose leaves are edged with golden-yellow

E. x *e.* 'Limelight', whose dark green leaves have a central blotch of yellow and pale green

This species is also described in the section on exposed gardens. (See p 22.)

Elaeagnus pungens 'Maculata'

Elaeagnus pungens 'Maculata' is a lovely, variegated shrub but it does have a habit of reverting, so trim it regularly to keep the variegation. A hedge of *E. p.* 'Maculata' could certainly be used to lighten a dreary boundary.

Eucalyptus gunnii (cider gum)

One of the hardiest of the genus, this species has the most beautiful silvery blue-green, aromatic leaves. It responds well to hard clipping and makes an unusually coloured hedge. In warmer areas, particularly around the Mediterranean, *E. gunnii* is often used for hedges and the perfume from the leaves when the hot sun has been on them is quite overpowering, especially after a brief shower of rain.

Griselinia littoralis

This shrub is included here because of its lovely, glossy, evergreen leaves. It is a naturally tall-growing plant which responds well to clipping and makes a light, graceful hedge. *Griselinia littoralis* has been described in more detail in the section on sheltered coastal gardens (see p 26).

Ilex aquifolium (common holly)

This holly is included here as it is often used in indigenous hedges where its evergreen properties

Eucalyptus gunnii (cider gum)

thicken and enliven an otherwise deciduous hedge. Interweaving variegated hollies with other hedging plants gives an interesting tapestry effect. *Ilex aquifolium* has been described in more detail in the section on windy sites. (See p 29).

Laurus nobilis (bay laurel)

This is the shrub that produces the bay leaf. It is often grown purely for its culinary uses but will stand clipping hard to form a hedge, particularly in coastal areas, where there is less likelihood of frost: it is on the tender side so will not withstand exposed, cold areas. *Laurus nobilis* is also used for topiary to form pyramidal shapes.

Ligustrum ovalifolium 'Aureum'

Ligustrum spp. (privet)

Long associated with urban gardens, this plant responds well to the shears. I have included it here although in cold areas it is considered to be semi-evergreen. It is very vigorous, with profuse clusters of creamy, fragrant flowers in midsummer, but dies back during winter. Fast growing, it makes a dense, sturdy hedge. It does tend to rob the surrounding soil of nutrients so care is needed in siting if other plants are to be positioned near it. For dense hedges of ligustrum it is best to plant a staggered double row with 15in (38cm) between the rows and 18in (45cm) between the plants. For a more slender hedge of 3–12ft (1–3.6m) high, plant 12–15in (30–38cm) apart. The species listed below make good dense hedges.

Ligustrum japonica (Japanese privet)

Ligustrum japonica has dense, dark, glossy leaves – not unlike camellia leaves – with large, creamy-white flowers in late summer.

Ligustrum ovalifolium

Ligustrum ovalifolium is also known as the green privet. It is a small-leaved, evergreen shrub which is often used for formal clipped hedges.

Ligustrum ovalifolium 'Aureum'

Ligustrum ovalifolium 'Aureum' is deemed to be semi-evergreen. It has medium-sized, glossy, variegated leaves of bright gold and green. It is a less vigorous plant than *L. ovalifolium*.

Ligustrum vulgare

Ligustrum vulgare, the wild privet, is similar to *L. ovalifolium* but has long bunches of shining black fruits in autumn which add to the autumn food store for birds.

Prunus spp. (laurel)

Laurel hedges are often used in larger suburban gardens and laurel is also a very popular hedging

Prunus lusitanica (Portugal laurel)

plant in provincial French towns. Because of its dense, protective growth it makes a popular nesting area for blackbirds and thrushes, so it also plays a role in the support of wildlife.

Prunus laurocerasus (cherry laurel)

This shrub has been described more fully in the section on windy sites (see p 30), but the fact that cherry laurel is evergreen and responds well to regular, formal clipping, makes it very useful and therefore worthy of an entry in this section.

Prunus laurocerasus can be used in any number of locations and conditions. Once it is established it will tolerate dry shade but it does need moisture until its root system is well formed. Cherry laurel can be pruned by hand, using secateurs, if it is not too large. This gives the hedge a very crisp but natural appearance.

Prunus lusitanica (Portugal laurel)

This laurel has dark green, oval leaves with red stems. Its sprays of fragrant cream flowers in early summer are followed in autumn by red fruits which turn to purple. It is a very hardy shrub and forms a dense, interesting hedge. This laurel has also been described in the section on windy sites (see p 30).

Quercus ilex (holm oak)

One of the most handsome evergreen trees, this will respond to clipping to form large, formal hedges. It has dark, leathery, shiny leaves which are often grey on the underside, and its yellow catkins in early summer are a picture. It will thrive in good, well-drained, fertile soil. However, it is not suitable for cold, exposed areas so coastal regions and the warmer climates of the British Isles are its favourite habitat – a hedge of *Quercus ilex* will withstand a coastal wind.

Flowers and fragrance

MIXING AND MATCHING

This section includes a particularly interesting mix of hedge plants. Hedges can be made up of one plant, giving a uniformity of colour and fragrance, or can be a little more imaginative, with 'mixed and matched' plants. I will deal with the fragrant flowering plants in two groups, the larger hedging plants and the ones which can be used for small, neat hedges or indeed, just edges. The following plants are particularly good to use for a uniform hedge where fragrance is an added bonus.

ABOVE *Santolina chamaecyparissus*

LEFT *Hydrangea macrophylla* 'Mariesii'

LARGER HEDGES
Flowering and fragrant

Buddleja spp.
Buddleja davidii cvs
Choisya ternata
Crataegus monogyna
Elaeagnus x *ebbingei*
Genista hispanica (see p 23)
Mahonia aquifolium
Malus huphensis

Osmanthus delavayi
Philadelphus spp.
Philadelphus coronarius
Philadelphus inodorus var. *grandiflorus*
Philadelphus x *lemoinei*
Pittosporum tobira
Prunus lusitanica
Rosa spp. (see pp 64–73)

Spartium junceum
Syringa spp.
Syringa x *chinensis*
Syringa x *persica*
Syringa villosa
Ulex europaeus
Viburnum tinus

LARGER HEDGES

Flowering and fragrant

Buddleja spp.

There are over 100 species of this wonderful shrub giving a range of colourful racemes in the summer. They are a must for environmentally friendly gardeners as they are very attractive to butterflies.

Buddlejas are mostly deciduous in Britain and need to be cut back fairly hard in early spring to encourage the new growth on which they flower. Some cultivars are perfect for making colourful screens, if correctly sited, but they are not suitable for more formal hedges. Buddlejas are often found in town gardens – they don't appear to object to polluted air – but take care in siting them: they can grow very tall if they are not pruned in early spring to keep them within bounds.

Buddleja davidii 'Black Knight'

Buddleja davidii cvs (butterfly bush)

This is tolerant of most soils and situations but does best in full sun. *Buddleja davidii* is probably the most popular species for using as a screen, and it is well suited to coastal regions. Its beautiful long racemes, with fragrant flowers, appear from midsummer to early autumn. The following cultivars are easily obtainable from most good nurseries and garden centres:

B. d. 'Black Knight', very dark purple flowers
B. d. 'Fortune', soft lilac flowers with an orange eye
B. d. 'Royal Red', dark crimson-purple flowers

Choisya ternata (Mexican orange blossom)

This shrub is also grown for its very fragrant, star-like, creamy flowers which bloom from late spring through to autumn. It is happy in sun or partial shade but does need a sheltered spot. It makes an informal, evergreen hedge.

Crataegus monogyna (hawthorn)

Crataegus monogyna is described in the section on traditional hedgerows, but it must be included here also because of its very distinctive blossom which heralds late spring. (See p 16.)

Elaeagnus x ebbingei

This fast-growing evergreen shrub makes a wonderful, dense hedge and the silvery underside of the leaves gives a lightness of touch. Its scented, creamy flowers bloom from early spring right through to summer. This species has also been described in the sections on exposed gardens and evergreens (see pp 22 and 42).

Mahonia aquifolium (Oregon grape)

The most popular mahonia species for hedging is *Mahonia aquifolium*, commonly known as Oregon grape. It is evergreen with dark, bronze green leaves which turn to a dark purple-red in autumn. It has sweetly scented yellow flowers in late winter

Malus huphensis (Chinese crab apple)

and early spring, making it invaluable for the winter garden. The fruits, which follow from midsummer onwards, add interest later in the season. Because of its prickly leaves, the hedge makes a good protective boundary; it is often used in town gardens because of this quality. It has a suckering habit so thickens well if just lightly trimmed to keep it in shape.

Malus huphensis (Chinese crab apple)

The Chinese crab apple makes an unusual hedge and can be pruned to stay around 6–8ft (2–2.5m) in height. It really wants to grow into a tree but in the right location its dense spring and summer foliage, together with its perfumed, white flowers, makes a wonderful screen. It could be used to separate a kitchen garden from the main areas of a garden or planted beside paths. The fruit remains

on the branches well into the autumn and the leaves also give vibrant autumn colour. With constant pruning the twiggy branches weave well into each other and, although deciduous, the hedge stays very dense even during the winter months, so it could be used successfully in areas where some privacy is required.

Osmanthus delavayi

This is another good, sturdy, evergreen plant, though fairly slow growing. Its lovely, perfumed, cream flowers show from mid- to late spring. It will only grow to around 6–8ft (2–2.5m) in height. Used near a regularly trodden path or close to the door of the house, its perfume is a real bonus. It does not mind being cut back regularly, and can also be grown as a specimen shrub.

Philadelphus 'Virginal'

Philadelphus spp.
This must be one of the most highly perfumed plants whether grown as a hedge or as a specimen shrub. Its scent fills the air from late spring to midsummer and its flowers, regardless of species, are always beautiful. Philadelphus species make some of the best white hedges and will thrive in most soils and conditions. *Philadelphus* 'Virginal', one of the most popular cultivars, has masses of heavily perfumed, double white flowers.

Philadelphus coronarius (mock orange)
An ideal species for hedging, *P. coronarius* has small, sweetly scented flowers.

Philadelphus inodorus var. *grandiflorus*
Philadelphus inodorus var. *grandiflorus* has large, single white flowers which are not quite so heavily scented, but it is a vigorous shrub.

Pittosporum tobira (Japanese pittosporum, mock orange)
This lovely, glossy evergreen shrub is included here because its cream flowers, which appear in long sprays in late spring and mellow to yellow through the summer months, are very fragrant.

It is an extremely versatile plant and if a large evergreen hedge is the order of the day, then the perfumed flowers are an added bonus. However, it is not very hardy so would only be suitable for southern areas of England, particularly coastal areas.

It is used frequently in the south of France and temperate Mediterranean climates in much the same way as laurel is used in Britain, clipped neatly into crisp hedges at a variety of heights. *Pittosporum tobira* is also described in the section on sheltered coastal gardens (see p 27).

Prunus lusitanica (Portugal laurel)

I have included this evergreen shrub here because of its scented white flowers which appear in long slender racemes in early summer. It is an extremely versatile hedging plant not only because of its evergreen qualities but also because its red stems and fragrant flowers add interest. *Prunus lusitanica* is also described in the section on evergreens (see p 45).

Spartium junceum (Spanish broom)

This plant's wind-resistant qualities make it ideal in seaside or coastal areas. It is one of the most vividly coloured hedging plants and also has a very strong perfume. Its golden flowers last from midsummer to early autumn. This species is more fully described in the section on exposed gardens (see p 25).

Syringa spp. (lilac)

We usually think of lilacs as specimen trees with their magnificent racemes of highly perfumed flowers. However, they can be pruned back in much the same way as *Malus huphensis* to restrict and control their growth. They do make large hedges and, as they are greedy feeders, need to be kept moist and well-manured to produce flowers, so a top dressing is necessary during the winter months. Their flowers are produced in early spring and can range in colour from white right through to the darkest purples and magentas. The species listed below are particularly suitable for hedges.

Syringa x chinensis (Rouen lilac)

Rouen lilac can reach 10ft (3m). It produces long, drooping, light purple flowers in late spring.

Syringa x persica (Persian lilac)

Syringa x *persica* will grow to 6ft (2m) and is the most compact species of the lilacs. It is slender in growth and has light purple flowers which appear in early summer. There is also a white cultivar available – *S.* x *p.* 'Alba'.

Syringa villosa

This lilac will also reach 10ft (3m). It produces racemes of pale pink-lilac flowers in early summer.

Ulex europaeus (gorse)

This is another seaside shrub. Its perfumed, pea-like, yellow flowers are reminiscent, in both appearance and fragrance, of broom. *Ulex europaeus* is described in more detail in the section on specific conditions (see p 25).

Viburnum tinus

This evergreen hedging shrub has flat heads of heavily scented, creamy white flowers which appear from late winter to early summer. These are followed by shiny black berries in autumn. They will thrive in most conditions and are one of the very few winter-flowering shrubs.

Syringa x *persica* (Persian lilac)

LARGER HEDGES
Flowering but without fragrance

Abelia x *grandiflora*
Berberis spp.
Berberis darwinii
Berberis julianae
Berberis x *ottawensis* 'Superba'
Berberis sanguinea
Berberis x *stenophylla*
Berberis thunbergii cvs
Ceanothus thyrsiflorus var. *repens*
Chaenomeles spp.
Chaenomeles cathayensis
Chaenomeles speciosa cvs
Chaenomeles x *superba* cvs
Corylus avellana
Corylus maxima 'Purpurea'
Cotoneaster spp.
Cotoneaster divaricatus
Cotoneaster franchetii
Cotoneaster simonsii
Deutzia spp.
Deutzia longifolia 'Veitchii'
Deutzia scabra 'Flore Pleno'

Forsythia spp.
Fuchsia spp. (see p 26)
Hebe spp. (see p 26)
Hippophae rhamnoides (see p 23)
Hydrangea macrophylla cvs
Hypericum x *moserianum* (see p 32)
Kalmia latifolia (see p 35)
Kerria japonica
Olearia spp. (see p 23)
Potentilla spp.
Potentilla fruticosa
Pyracantha cvs
Rhododendron ponticum (see p 35)
Ribes alpinum (see p 32)
Spiraea spp.
Spiraea japonica 'Anthony Waterer'
Spiraea thunbergii
Symphoricarpos albus var. *laevigatus* (see p 32)
Tamarix spp. (see p 25)
Weigela spp.
Weigela florida

Flowering but without fragrance

There are a number of shrubs which have no significant fragrance but whose flowers add a riot of colour to a thick hedge.

Abelia x grandiflora

This lovely arching shrub makes large, rounded hedges reaching about 5ft (1.5m). It is evergreen but is susceptible to cold so may die back in colder winters. It has glossy dark green foliage and a mass of tiny pink flowers in late summer. Light pruning will keep it in trim.

Berberis spp.

Berberis is another large genus with a number of species suitable for hedging. These plants form very prickly, protective hedges as well as providing flowers, autumn colour and berries. They are very adaptable plants and will grow in any soil, in sun or in shade. The following species are the most popular for hedges.

Berberis darwinii

This handsome early flowering shrub has shiny, dark green leaves with rich orange flowers followed by blue berries. For hedges 4–7ft (1–2m) high, plant about 2ft (60cm) apart.

Berberis julianae

Upright, semi-evergreen and prickly with lemon yellow flowers (very slightly fragrant) followed by blue-black fruits. Good protective hedge.

Berberis x ottawensis 'Superba' (syn. B. x o. 'Purpurea'

Medium to large and vigorous, with yellow spring flowers, red autumn fruits and purple-red foliage.

Berberis sanguinea

This is a compact, medium-sized, evergreen shrub with neat growth which makes it ideal for hedges. The leaves are grey-green and oval.

Berberis x stenophylla

This shrub is evergreen and has a lovely, arching growth habit. Yellow flowers clothe its branches from mid- to late spring. After flowering, it must be pruned with secateurs to keep it in shape. Berberis x stenophylla makes a glorious, glowing hedge in spring.

Berberis thunbergii cvs

This plant forms a dense, prickly, deciduous hedge. Its small, yellow spring flowers are followed by red berries. The leaves turn bright red in autumn, giving a wonderful splash of colour. For hedges of 3–4ft (1–1.2m), plant at 2ft (60cm) intervals.

Berberis thunbergii 'Atropurpurea Nana', a dwarf form, makes a neat, compact hedge of rich purple

Berberis julianae

foliage; the foliage turns even darker as autumn progresses. *Berberis thunbergii* f. *atropurpurea* is a somewhat larger form, but still with the rich red-purple foliage.

Ceanothus thyrsiflorus var. repens

Ceanothus are mostly evergreen shrubs. There is a wide variety of species belonging to this genus, nearly all of which have prolific blue flowers which appear during early summer.

However, only *Ceanothus thyrsiflorus* var. *repens* is really suitable for hedging, forming a loose, arching hedge. It likes well-drained, light soil in fairly sheltered positions, which generally restricts it to warmer gardens.

Chaenomeles spp.

This plant, clipped tightly to the old wood, can make a very beautiful low hedge, full of flower from mid- to late spring. Fruits, often a pink-golden colour, form in autumn and can be used to make quince jelly. The dark red species are the most commonly grown.

Chaenomeles cathayensis

Chaenomeles cathayensis has the most prominent thorns of all – making it a good species for a protective hedge – though it is more sparsely branched than many of the other species. It produces lovely salmon pink flowers.

Chaenomeles speciosa cvs

Chaenomeles speciosa 'Moerloosei' is a lovely pale pink variety and *C. s.* 'Nivalis', a pure white cultivar, is also extremely prickly so can be used to form a beautiful, strong protective hedge.

Chaenomeles x superba cvs

Of the various *Chaenomeles* x *superba* cultivars 'Boule de Feu' is particularly popular as is the rich orange-red *C.* x *s.* 'Knapp Hill Scarlet'.

Ceanothus thyrsiflorus var. *repens*

Corylus avellana (cobnut)

I have included *Corylus avellana* in this section because of its beautiful yellow catkins which, in late winter, hang like little lambs' tails all over the slender branches. These produce cobnuts in the winter months. Corylus is indigenous to Britain and is often planted in a traditional mixed country hedge. The leaves which follow the catkins turn yellow in autumn, providing vibrant colour.

Corylus maxima 'Purpurea' (filbert)

Corylus maxima 'Purpurea' is a purple-leaved form of the filbert, usually grown for the large nuts it produces in winter. It is suitable for clipping to produce a formal hedge and provides a lovely contrast with the common hazel if the two are grown together.

Cotoneaster spp.

Cotoneasters are very obliging plants; they will grow in almost any soil and in any position. Their flowers are particularly attractive to bees and their winter berries are a reliable source of food for wildlife. These well-known shrubs sport three particularly good hedging varieties, listed below.

Cotoneaster divaricatus

This species forms a quick-growing hedge with glossy, dark green leaves, tiny white flowers, which appear in mid- and late summer and a multitude of red berries in autumn.

Cotoneaster franchetii

Cotoneaster franchetii can reach 8ft (2.5m), and has an arching character. Its rich green leaves are backed with silver.

Cotoneaster simonsii

Cotoneaster simonsii is semi-evergreen. It has dark green leaves, cream flowers, which appear in early and mid-summer, large scarlet berries and wonderful autumn colour. This species can grow to 8ft (2.5m), and is suitable for narrow areas as it does not grow very wide.

Deutzia spp.

These hardy shrubs can make lovely hedges as their flowers of pink or pink-and-white bloom throughout early and midsummer. They are also versatile, as they will grow in any well-drained, fertile soil, in sun or partial shade.

Deutzia longifolia 'Veitchii'

This deciduous cultivar has long, narrow leaves and clusters of mauve flowers, tinged with pink, in early and midsummer. It will grow into a good, medium-sized shrub of up to 6ft (1.8m).

Deutzia scabra 'Flore Pleno'

This upright, deciduous shrub will grow to 10ft (3m). It has dark green, narrow oval leaves and dense clusters of double white flowers which are tinged with mauve-pink.

Forsythia spp.

This is one of the first brilliantly coloured hedges to herald early spring. Its glorious, bright yellow flowers cheer up the gloomiest of days and the darkest of corners. Suitable for almost any soil and any position, the following three species are particularly suitable for hedging:

F. x *intermedia* 'Spectabilis' has a deep golden hue

F. vitellina is more twiggy in growth

F. viridissima flowers later in mid-spring and is a paler shade of yellow

Hydrangea macrophylla cvs

These beautiful shrubs are suitable for large hedges or screens. They grow particularly well in coastal areas and in larger town gardens. The species is divided into two groups: hortensias (also known as mopheads), which have dense, domed heads, and lacecaps, which have open, flat heads. There are so many cultivars of this species, I suggest you read a more detailed book for further information. Toni Lawson-Hall and Brian Rothera's *Hydrangeas: A Garden Guide* will make you want to find space in your garden for them all. Suffice it to say that when

Cotoneaster franchetii

Hydrangea macrophylla 'Mariesii'

planted in areas with a reasonable amount of space, they add an almost translucent element of colour to the garden. In alkaline soils the blue varieties maintain their colour but on most soils, and particularly on chalk, the blue hydrangeas flower pink or pink-purple.

Hydrangeas need judicious pruning to keep them compact and free-flowering. Cut back the flowering stems to just above the uppermost bud in late spring, after the last frost. Young hydrangeas do not require much pruning in their early years but should they start to grow out of shape, cut the offending stems back to the ground. Again, always do this after any fear of frost. On older bushes, remove old or damaged wood during mild periods in mid- or late winter: this will encourage new growth from the base of the stem.

The following is a very small selection of the more well-known cultivars of *Hydrangea macrophylla:*

Hortensias (mopheads)
'Goliath' has deep pink flowers
'La France' has large pink to mid-blue flowers
'Madame Emile Mouillère' has lovely white flowers

Lacecaps
'Blue Wave' has blue flowers on acid soil
'Lanarth White' has white flowers
'Mariesii' has rose pink flowers

Banks of hydrangeas are very attractive when mixed with *Fuchsia magellanica,* and the grey leaves of *Olearia* x *haastii* and *O. macrodonta* make a subtle backdrop to the blues and pinks of these romantic shrubs.

Kerria japonica

This graceful shrub, which can reach 6½ft (2m) in a sheltered position, is more suited for use as a screen than a formal hedge. Its arching branches carry bright yellow, often double flowers from mid- to late spring. The cultivar, *Kerria japonica* 'Variegata', with cream markings on its leaves, is particularly pleasing. This shrub can be pruned and thinned after flowering but does need care in siting to ensure that it remains within bounds, as its suckering habit makes it somewhat invasive. Just as forsythia lightens up the garden earlier in the spring, so will kerria if placed in a shady spot. It will grow in most soils, in sun or partial shade.

Potentilla spp.

The potentilla genus includes many species which flower in a variety of colours. Most reputable garden centres and nurseries stock a good selection of shrubby potentillas as they are such versatile plants. More often than not, these are grown as specimen shrubs.

Potentilla fruticosa

Potentilla fruticosa is a hardy, dwarf to medium-sized shrub, tolerant of any soil or situation. It can reach 5ft (1.5m) in height but clipped lightly, will form a loose, informal hedge, providing a soft, feathery foliage and yellow flowers from early summer to late autumn. Although it is shade tolerant, most of the cultivars prefer to grow in a sunny spot; the more brightly coloured examples, such as *P. f.* 'Red Ace', prefer a little shade, as this keeps the colours vibrant.

Pyracantha cvs (firethorn)

These very spiny, prickly plants make good protective hedges as well as providing flowers and berries. They are not fussy about soil conditions or where they are planted. They produce masses of small creamy hawthorn-like flowers in late spring, followed by a wealth of brightly coloured berries in autumn – a good source of food for wildlife.

As they are evergreen and flowering, I am always surprised that they are not more widely used for hedging. I have seen the more columnar cultivars *P. coccinea* 'Red Column' and *P.* 'Teton' growing like sentinels either side of a front door, set off beautifully by the white weatherboard walls. Both of these species can be clipped into neat columns and will provide a mass of bright red and yellow-orange berries respectively, in the autumn.

All pyracanthas have toothed, dark green leaves and their branches can be cut back into shape after flowering, in the late summer. If pruned well at this time, they make a dense hedge which can be quite impenetrable. Another common feature is that they are very shade tolerant. Many of the modern varieties have been bred to be disease-resistant, as they have had a reputation for being prone to fireblight and canker.

There is a wide variety of pyracanthas available in garden centres, the majority of which can be used

Kerria japonica

for hedges or screens. The most popular varieties are listed below.

P. 'Golden Charmer' is an arching plant with large, orange-yellow berries

P. 'Mohave' makes a large, dense shrub with orange-red berries

P. 'Orange Glow' has a dense, vigorous habit and orange-red berries

P. 'Watereri' is a very good fruiting variety with bright red berries

Spiraea spp.

Spiraea is a large genus and many of its species make excellent flowering hedges. They are easy to grow, being tolerant of most conditions, though they do prefer a sunny spot. Their flowers range from white to crimson.

Spiraea japonica 'Anthony Waterer'

This dwarf cultivar is very popular for low hedges. It has bright crimson flowers.

Spiraea thunbergii

This very popular, early flowering species has a mass of white flowers in clusters along its branches from early to late spring. It has a dense habit but is small to medium-sized so will make an attractive, lower-growing hedge. Its foliage becomes tinted in autumn, which is an added bonus, but it is deciduous.

Weigela spp.

Weigelas are another very accommodating group of plants which enjoy most soils and are tolerant of sun or shade. Lovely trumpet flowers are their best feature and these can range from white to pale pinks and dark reds; there are also some varieties which sport yellow and cream flowers. The variegated species, with its cream-edged leaves, adds another dimension to the flowering hedge.

Weigelas can reach 6½ft (2m) in height and are ideal for screens. The tubular flowers appear from late spring to early summer and flower on the previous year's wood. They need to be thinned out and cut back immediately after flowering in order to maintain their shape and a good profusion of flowers the next year.

There are many cultivars of the genus and most good garden centres and nurseries offer a wide selection of weigelas. One particular cultivar that is worthy of note is *Weigela* 'Abel Carrière', a very free-flowering plant whose crimson-red blooms add a vivid touch to a hedge. Another is *Weigela* 'Florida Variegata', a lovely plant with cream-edged leaves and tubular, pink flowers. It is one of the more compact varieties.

Weigela florida

Weigela florida, also the parent of many cultivars, is a medium-sized shrub with reddish-pink, funnel-shaped flowers and oval leaves.

SMALLER HEDGES
Flowering and fragrant

Artemisia abrotanum
Lavandula spp.
Lavandula angustifolia 'Hidcote'
Lavandula angustifolia 'Munstead'
Lavandula angustifolia 'Rosea'
Lavandula x *intermedia* 'Grappenhall'
Rosmarinus officinalis
Santolina spp.
Santolina chamaecyparissus
Sarcococca confusa
Teucrium spp.
Teucrium chamaedrys
Teucrium fruticans

Lavender and its uses

Where lavender is grown as a crop for use in perfumes, the flower spikes will be harvested at their peak. Lavender grows well on the terraced hillsides around Grasse, in the Alpes Maritimes in southern France, and has been used as a basis for perfume since the seventeenth century. Ears of ripe lavender are also used to fill calico or cotton bags. It also grows well in other parts of Provence where the sunshine ripens the flowers just as it does the grapes grown in the region.

Lavender was introduced into England by the Romans who used it to perfume their bath water. Monks then planted it in monastic herb gardens, but it was not until Elizabethan times that we learnt more about its uses. Because of its strong fragrance it was widely used as a strewing herb to combat bad odours. The oil distilled from lavender for the perfume industry is also used in aromatherapy because its soothing and calming properties help to relieve headaches and induce sleep.

SMALLER HEDGES

Flowering and fragrant

The plants listed here, usually associated with small hedges or screens, lend themselves beautifully to herb gardens, potagers or divisions within kitchen or rose gardens. These plants all have fragrant flowers and often have aromatic leaves.

Artemisia abrotanum (southernwood or old man)

This old-fashioned herb only reaches 2–3ft (60–100cm) and can be kept very low by judicious pruning. It needs to be cut back hard in late spring to achieve a dense growth. Do not prune it hard during the winter even if it does look very straggly: you will kill it. After the last frost, prune it back to a good pair of buds, low on the stems of the new wood. Its aromatic, silvery foliage can produce very small, yellow flowers but these are rare in Britain. The fragrance is strong and the feathery leaves can be used sparingly to flavour salads. It also makes a very good herby, aromatic vinegar.

Lavandula spp. (lavender)

Lavandula is a very large genus with many different species all of which enjoy very similar situations. Lavenders need well-drained, light soil in open, sunny positions. To maintain the appearance of the foliage and encourage flowering, they should be clipped back to the previous season's growth once the flowering spikes are spent. This usually occurs in late summer.

For all of those listed, to achieve the required density, plants should be placed 12–15in (30–40cm) apart. They should be trimmed in mid-spring to tidy them up after winter ravages, then cut back fairly hard after flowering has peaked in late summer. It is absolutely essential to be ruthless with lavender or it will grow into a woody, straggly plant, the shape of the hedge will be lost, and there will be a decline in flowers.

Although lavender originated in the Mediterranean countries, English lavender is one of the mainstays of English cottage gardens and is regularly used in conjunction with roses. Lavender makes beautiful hedges for kitchen gardens and neat dividing hedges or edges for parterres and herb gardens. There is a wide selection of lavenders; the following varieties make particularly good hedges.

Lavandula angustifolia 'Hidcote' (syn. L. 'Hidcote Blue')

This evergreen lavender has silver-grey, narrow leaves and masses of violet-blue flower spikes from midsummer to early autumn. It derives its name from Lawrence Johnston's beautiful Cotswold garden Hidcote Manor where it is used extensively. This lavender is suitable for low hedges of up to 2ft (60cm) in height.

Lavandula angustifolia 'Munstead' (syn. L. 'Rosea')

This is another low-growing, compact lavender with narrow, grey-green leaves and very distinctive deep purple flowers.

Lavandula angustifolia 'Rosea'

This lavender differs in that its flowers, as the name suggests, are a soft pink hue and its leaves are slightly greener than the purple lavenders. I have grown this cultivar in a small herb garden to edge a bed of purple sage and it looked very pretty indeed. It is compact in habit.

Lavandula x intermedia 'Grappenhall'

This is a more robust form with fairly broad, grey-green leaves and lavender-blue flowers. *Lavandula* x *intermedia* 'Grappenhall' can reach 5ft (1.5m) in height and has strong flowering stems. It is ideal for larger hedging borders or grown against stone walls to soften the contours.

Rosmarinus officinalis (rosemary)

Rosemary is one of the most popular herbs. It has rather sticky, aromatic, narrow green leaves and fragrant blue flowers which appear along the branches of the old wood in late spring and continue to bloom intermittently until the autumn. There is also a pink cultivar, *Rosmarinus officinalis* 'Roseus', which has delicate pink flowers. It responds well to hard clipping which makes it suitable for hedges. Once well established, these plants can make dense hedges of between 2–4ft (60–120cm) in height. However, it is important to remember that they need a well-drained, sunny spot and do not grow well in cold, exposed, damp sites.

Santolina spp. (cotton lavender)

These plants are often called cotton lavender and, like true lavenders, hail from the Mediterranean. They make wonderful evergreen mounds of silvery grey-green growth. The leaves are aromatic, deeply indented and woolly to the touch. If left to their own devices they produce small, fragrant, yellow pompom flowers on tall stems. Santolina makes a good, compact, low-growing hedge for herb gardens and potagers or to front borders edging walkways. To keep the hedge in a neat shape, clip off the flowering spikes as soon as they appear, just as you would lavender.

Santolina chamaecyparissus

This is the most popular cultivar for dwarf hedging and has been in existence since Elizabethan times. It was thought that French gardeners introduced the plant to the English Court when they brought

Rosemary and its uses

In warm regions, like the south of France, rosemary is grown among the shrubberies in cultivated gardens and in the wild where the hot sun releases its strong aromatic perfume.
I have also seen it used regularly for planting in parterre gardens and for topiary – its growth gives lovely shapes under the shears of an expert topiarist. I grew a wonderful rosemary bush just outside my kitchen door, in a well-drained, sunny, south-facing border, and clipped it into the shape of a large pompom. I used it so much in cooking

that I rarely needed to attack it with the shears. Rosemary is steeped in myth and folklore. In Elizabethan times betrothed couples would carry sprigs of rosemary as symbols of their fidelity to each other and, like lavender, it was widely used as a strewing herb to combat unpleasant odours.
It was also burnt in rooms where there was illness as it was believed that the fragrant smoke would cleanse and purify the air. Today, rosemary oil is used to perfume soaps, room fresheners and sprays for use in a similar way.

their skills in creating knot gardens. In southern France, where it grows wild, flowers are sometimes collected, dried, and used to make a very strong, distinctive chamomile or manzanilla tea. It requires the same conditions as lavender and rosemary.

Sarcococca confusa (sweet box)

This delightful evergreen shrub grows to about 18in (45cm) in height. It has lovely, glossy green leaves all year round and tassel-like, fragrant, cream flowers from midwinter to early spring. It does not like exposed, windy sites as the wind will scorch the shiny leaves, but in a more sheltered spot it is a joy, particularly for its winter fragrance. It can be clipped into a formal, low-growing hedge or, alternatively, makes a lovely container specimen.

Teucrium spp.

Along with artemisia, rosemary, and santolina, teucriums are particularly sensuous plants, having both aromatic leaves and fragrant flowers.

Teucrium chamaedrys

This very low-growing teucrium needs regular clipping to keep it neat. It grows to about 12in (30cm) and produces spiky pink flowers in midsummer, when its year-round fragrance becomes stronger – as with all fragrant plants, the heat of the sun releases its oils.

Like lavender and santolina, it has a life span of about five years and can become woody if not hard-pruned to encourage new growth after flowering.

Teucrium fruticans (tree germander, shrubby germander)

Teucrium fruticans is evergreen, fully hardy, and produces little blue flowers in summer. It enjoys a well-drained, sunny site and prefers a more alkaline than neutral soil if possible. Pruning with shears will improve its density of growth. If left alone it can reach 3–6½ft (1-2m), but with regular clipping it can be kept at any desired height. It is often used as a low hedge in potagers and kitchen gardens and is a very good plant for coastal hedges. It also has a culinary use – flavouring liqueurs.

COMBINING HEDGE PLANTS

There are no hard and fast rules about combining hedge plants. Personal taste and common sense dictate the patterns. An eye for colour and shape are the most frequently employed senses – if you like the combination, that is really all that matters. As regards common sense, the plants' individual requirements, along with their height and shape, must be taken into consideration.

Seaside and coastal areas

Escallonia rubra var. macrantha with Olearia macrodonta or O. x haastii

Escallonia rubra var. *macrantha*, very popular in coastal gardens, is a vigorous and free-flowering evergreen shrub which, when interplanted with *Olearia macrodonta* or *O. x haastii*, makes an interesting and colourful hedge.

The holly-like, grey-green leaves of *O. macrodonta*, and its clusters of white daisy-like flowers, are shown off to their best against the shiny, evergreen foliage of the escallonia and its sprays of bright red flowers. (*Olearia macrodonta* has larger leaves and broader panicles of flowers than *O. x haastii*.) Both of these olearias have a fairly upright and shrubby habit which enables them to grow into the escallonia with ease.

Olearia macrodonta or O. x haastii with Fuchsia magellanica

The upright habit of these olearias also works well when they are planted with *Fuchsia magellanica*. Again, the colour and growth patterns of these shrubs are very complementary as the striking red bell flowers of the fuchsia hang delicately among the grey-green leaves and white daisy flowers of the olearias. However, this combination should only be used in a sheltered coastal position as the fuchsia needs protection from really cold winds.

Fuchsia magellanica with Hydrangea macrophylla

Hydrangea macrophylla is often planted with *Fuchsia magellanica* and again, its upright habit supports and complements the arching sprays of the fuchsia. Remember, though, that both hydrangeas and fuchsias are deciduous, so expect a rather bare border throughout the winter months.

Hydrangea macrophylla in a mixed flowering hedge

Hydrangea macrophylla can also be used in a mixed flowering hedge to punctuate the hedge line randomly. The effect, when in full flower, is romantically informal as hydrangea flowers have a translucency which is enhanced by the brightness of a coastal background. An added advantage is that hydrangea leaves turn a variety of autumn colours before they fall and, as is so often found on the coast, the neighbouring brilliance of *Spartium junceum* (Spanish broom), with its golden-yellow, pea-like flowers from early summer onwards, makes a vibrant end to the autumn months.

Inland areas

Chaenomeles japonica with Viburnum tinus

This combination is particularly good as the chaenomeles needs the evergreen leaves of viburnum to set off its red flowers early in the year. The deciduous branches of the chaenomeles intertwine with each other to form a dense framework. The *Viburnum tinus* also looks attractive if planted at either end of the hedge, forming loose pillars of evergreen leaves and creamy pink flowers which throw the bare hedge into relief.

Berberis thunbergii 'Atropurpurea Nana' with Buxus sempervirens

Used to form a low, clipped hedge, this combination is ideal for edging a path or patio area. For a more formal hedge, plant a mixture of berberis with ligustrum or buxus and intersperse with narrow-growing conifers such as *Chamaecyparis lawsoniana* 'Columnaris' or *Juniperus chinensis* 'Pyramidalis', a slow-growing, dense, blue-green columnar bush.

Lavandula spp.

Mix lavenders together to give a fragrant and colourful edge to a rose garden or herbaceous bed. Try *Lavandula angustifolia* 'Hidcote' with *L. a.* 'Rosea'. This is less formal than planting in one colour, and works very well in a sunny, well-drained potager or parterre garden.

Fagus sylvatica with Fagus sylvatica f. purpurea

Planted alternately, these two plants will give a dramatic chequerboard effect, especially in autumn, when the *Fagus sylvatica* turns a wonderful rich golden colour.

Taxus baccata with Taxus baccata 'Aurea'

These dark green and golden yews can be planted in much the same way as above to create a dramatic effect in a large garden. Try interspersing such a hedge with *Taxus baccata* 'Fastigiata' (Irish yew). This very dark green yew has a dense, erect habit, and forms a broad column. Alternatively, intersperse with *Taxus baccata* 'Fastigiata Aureomarginata' which is very similar, but has a golden rim to its leaves. Plant at intervals along the hedge or at the apices.

Fagus sylvatica with *Fagus sylvatica* f. *purpurea*

Roses

THE VERSATILE ROSE

I have devoted a whole chapter to this genus as
there are innumerable species and varieties that can
be used for hedges. If you use your imagination and
check the growth patterns of the modern shrub
roses, floribundas, old-fashioned roses and, indeed,
even some of the small polyantha roses, there are
many that will lend themselves beautifully to
decorative and fragrant hedges. I have used the
little *R.* 'De Meaux' (syn. *R.* 'Rose de Meaux')
(a centifolia or many-petalled rose), clipped tightly
together to border a larger rose bed and I have seen
R. LA SÉVILLANA ('Meigekanu') (a floribunda or
cluster-flowered ground cover rose) make a
wonderful hedge of multi-blooms, repeating
throughout the summer.

ABOVE *Rosa* 'Pax'

LEFT *Rosa* 'Charles de Mills'

INDIGENOUS AND INFORMAL HEDGES

The indigenous hedgerow relies on some of the wild hedging roses to add interest, colour and perfume and these will also help to thicken a country hedge. Some are large, arching roses which can be used to grow over and between hedges, to cover banks or, in large plantings, as ground cover.

INDIGENOUS AND INFORMAL HEDGES
Species roses

R. canina cvs

R. pimpinellifolia (syn. *R. spinosissima*) cvs

R. rubiginosa (syn. *R. eglanteria*)

Species roses
Rosa canina (dog rose) cvs

Rosa canina, a shrub rose, is one of the most familiar of all the indigenous roses. *Rosa canina* 'Abbotswood', named and distributed by the well-known horticulturist Graham Stuart Thomas, is not quite so vigorous as *R. canina*. It has gently perfumed, pink, almost double flowers borne on long, arching branches. It can be used in the same way as its parent to thicken an informal hedge. I have described *R. canina* in the section on traditional hedgerows (see p 17).

Rosa pimpinellifolia (syn. *R. spinosissima*) cvs (Scotch rose, burnet rose)

The new stems of these dense shrubs are covered with prickles and light green, fern-like foliage. The flowers are pale yellow, small and single-petalled, with darker yellow stamens. They bloom in late spring and early summer and are followed by shiny, purple-black fruits in autumn. They will grow in

any dry, poor soil, suckering their way through the ground to give a dense thicket of stems. This quality makes them an ideal deterrent hedge. Unfortunately, they only flower once but their beauty more than compensates for their short display. *Rosa pimpinellifolia* 'Stanwell Perpetual' makes a lovely, soft, arching screen with medium-sized, double, pink and perfumed blooms for most of the summer.

Rosa rubiginosa (syn. *R. eglanteria*) (sweet briar, eglantine)

This is the common sweet briar or eglantine. It has an abundance of small, solitary, pale pink flowers amongst small, pinnate leaves. Sweet briar will tolerate poor soils and shade. It was often planted by early American settlers to form a protective hedge or screen. They chose this rose for many reasons: it was long-lived, it was particularly easy to propagate from seedlings, it had scented foliage and fragrant flowers, and finally, it produced abundant autumn hips.

Rosa canina (dog rose) cvs

Rosa 'Amy Robsart'

INDIGENOUS AND INFORMAL HEDGES
Cultivars

R. 'Amy Robsart'

R. 'Anne of Geierstein'

R. 'Manning's Blush'

R. 'Meg Merrilies'

Cultivars
Rubiginosa hybrid roses (hybrid sweet briar)

These beautifully fragrant, arching roses have evolved from the wild form of the sweet briar or eglantine rose. They produce a mass of thorns and their resultant impenetrability is a great bonus when they are used to form a hedge. Like their wild ancestors, they have soft green foliage and attractive, perfumed flowers, followed by autumn hips. The following rubiginosa hybrid roses have a strong affinity to the sweet briar and can be used in large planting displays as part of a screen or large hedge, or as single specimen roses. All are followed by large hips in the autumn and will make a dense hedge if pruned in spring.

Rosa 'Amy Robsart'

With its prickly stems and vigorous habit, this rose is particularly spectacular when in flower: it produces a mass of semi-double, deep pink, fragrant flowers in early summer. However, it only blooms once in the season so it can appear rather dull until autumn, when its branches become covered in hips. 'Amy Robsart' can reach around 10 x 8ft (3 x 2.5m).

Rosa 'Anne of Geierstein'

This vigorous rose has scented flowers and foliage. Single flowers with dark red petals and a golden centre are followed by bright red hips. It also reaches around 10 x 8ft (3 x 2.5m) so is suitable for larger spaces.

Rosa 'Manning's Blush'

This has similar features to the varieties listed above but is more compact. It has scented foliage and very small, double white flowers, flushed pink in bud. With its densely arching branches it makes a lovely soft, informal hedge around 4–5ft (1.2–1.5m) high.

Rosa 'Meg Merrilies'

This is a very prickly, vigorous rose with fragrant, dark crimson flowers and scented foliage. It grows to around 8 x 7ft (2.5 x 2m).

Rosa foetida 'Bicolor' (syn. *Rosa* 'Austrian Copper')

INTERNAL, LOW-GROWING AND OTHER TYPES OF HEDGE
Species roses

R. arvensis
R. foetida 'Bicolor' (syn. R. 'Austrian Copper')
R. moyesii
R. multiflora
R. virginiana
R. xanthina f. hugonis (syn. R. hugonis)

INTERNAL, LOW-GROWING AND OTHER TYPES OF HEDGE

Species roses
Rosa arvensis

This vigorous ground-cover rose can be used to grow through hedges in the same way as the indigenous roses. It has single, creamy-white and very beautiful flowers.

Rosa foetida 'Bicolor' (syn. *Rosa* 'Austrian Copper')

In full flower this shrub rose is brilliantly coloured; the single, bright red flowers have yellow on the reverse side of their petals, hence the name. It is an old rose and will clip into shape if required. For an interesting internal hedge, this would certainly be a different choice. It is quite low growing, reaching around 5 x 4ft (1.5 x 1.2m).

Rosa moyesii

I have used this shrub rose to form a screen edging a circular drive in order to conceal approaching cars from the lawn area. It can grow to 10ft (3m) and is extremely thorny. Its lax branches carry single, dark red flowers with golden stamens, followed in autumn by large, flagon-shaped, orange-red hips. It provides an informal screen and adds colour in summer and autumn.

Rosa multiflora

Another very old rose, this rambler rose can be used to scramble through hedges, formal or informal. It has a mass of single white flowers which are produced in long trusses. Its lovely glossy foliage is comparatively thornless.

Rosa virginiana

This species, which likes sandy soil, can make a dense hedge. It has light green foliage and small, single pink flowers with yellow stamens. It produces a mass of fat red hips which last well into winter and the leaves turn the most wonderful autumn colour. A medium-sized rose, it grows to about 5ft (1.5m).

Rosa xanthina f. hugonis (syn. *Rosa hugonis*)

Rosa xanthina f. *hugonis* has fern-like, green leaves with bright yellow flowers in late spring. It is one of the earliest roses to flower and is ideal for a spot that would benefit from an early show of colour. It can grow to over 7ft (2m) but can also be trimmed to keep it in shape.

Rosa virginiana

INTERNAL, LOW-GROWING AND OTHER TYPES OF HEDGE
Cultivars

R. x *alba* 'Alba Maxima'
    (syn. *R.* x *a.* 'Maxima', Jacobite rose, Cheshire rose)

R. x *alba* 'Alba Semiplena'
    (syn. *R.* x *a.* 'Semiplena')

R. 'Blanche Double de Coubert'

R. 'Charles de Mills'

R. 'De Meaux' (syn. *R.* 'Rose de Meaux')

R. 'Felicia'

R. 'Fru Dagmar Hastrup'

R. gallica 'Versicolor'
    (syn. *R. mundi*, *R. mundi* 'Versicolor')

R. 'Great Maiden's Blush'
    (*R.* cuisse de nymphe)

R. 'Gruss an Teplitz'

R. 'Hansa'

R. HERITAGE ('Ausblush')

R. 'Hermosa'

R. 'Ispahan'

R. JACQUELINE DU PRÉ ('Harwanna')

R. 'Madame Hardy'

R. MARJORIE FAIR ('Harhero')

R. 'Moonlight'

R. 'Nur Mahal'

R. x *odorata* 'Pallida'
    (syn. *R.* old blush China, *R.* Parson's pink China)

R. 'Pax'

R. 'Penelope'

R. 'Roseraie de l'Haÿ'

R. 'Schneezwerg' (syn. *R.* 'Snow Dwarf')

R. 'The Fairy' (syn. *R.* 'Fairy Rose')

R. 'Tuscany Superb'

R. WESTERLAND ('Korwest')

Cultivars

Alba roses

The Alba group includes some of the oldest roses, dating back to the fifteenth and sixteenth centuries. Their grey-green leaves are supported on vigorous upright stems. The three varieties listed below are particularly successful for hedging.

Rosa x *alba* 'Alba Maxima' (syn. *R.* x *a.* 'Maxima', Jacobite rose, Cheshire rose)

This rose is multi-petalled, and creamy white with reddish hips. The foliage has good autumn colour. It grows to around 6 x 5ft (1.8 x 1.5m).

Rosa x *alba* 'Alba Semiplena' (syn. *R.* x *a.* 'Semiplena')

This is a pure-white rose with semi-double, fragrant flowers and lovely autumn hips. It grows to around 8 x 5ft (2.4 x 1.5m).

Rosa x *alba* 'Alba Semiplena' (syn. *R.* x *a.* 'Semiplena')

Rosa 'Great Maiden's Blush' (syn. *R. cuisse de nymphe*)

This is probably one of the oldest Alba roses, dating back to the fifteenth century. It has soft pink, double flowers surrounded by blue-grey leaves. Slightly smaller than the previous two roses, it grows to around 5 x 3ft (1.5 x 1m).

China roses

It was not until the eighteenth century, when East India traders found bushes of repeatedly flowering, crimson roses, that *R. chinensis* was brought to the West. The first famous China rose, old blush China, was brought back in 1752 and from this, the hybrid tea roses, which are also repeat flowering, were bred. China roses have had an enormous influence on rose breeding over the last 100 years.

There are three particular varieties in this group which are suitable for hedging.

Rosa x *odorata* 'Pallida' (syn. *R.* old blush China, *R.* Parson's pink China)

This would make a wonderful small hedge, reaching up to 3ft (1m). It has double flowers that are pale pink when young but darken with age, and flowers freely from summer to autumn.

Rosa 'Gruss an Teplitz'

Rosa 'Gruss an Teplitz' is a sturdy, arching rose. Its dark crimson flowers, borne in clusters, have a strong, spicy perfume. This rose can reach 6ft (1.8m) if clipped to form an informal hedge.

Rosa 'Hermosa'

A very compact, soft mauve-pink rose which produces rounded hips in autumn. It is often used for dwarf hedging as its compact, sturdy growth forms neat, low-growing hedges. It rarely reaches 3ft (1m), and can be kept to any height below this by regular trimming. It is particularly suited to the smaller garden.

Rosa gallica 'Versicolor' (syn. *R. mundi, R. m.* 'Versicolor')

Damask roses

This is another of the wonderful old rose groups, dating from Elizabethan times. Some varieties are repeat flowering, most are disease-resistant, and all have the wonderful damask fragrance. Two that are of particular note for hedging purposes are described below.

Rosa 'Madame Hardy'

Rosa 'Madame Hardy' is a climbing damask rose which dates from around 1832. It is a particularly fragrant, pure white rose. It can grow to about 5 x 5ft (1.5 x 1.5m).

Rosa 'Ispahan'

The pink, semi-double flowers of *Rosa* 'Ispahan' have a long flowering season. It is a rose good for a smaller informal hedge as it grows only to around 4 x 3ft (1.2 x 1m).

Gallica roses

Some of the upright gallica roses can be planted together successfully to form a boundary or light screen. They are not dense roses but have large, beautiful flowers. There are three of particular note for hedging.

Rosa gallica 'Versicolor' (syn. *R. mundi, R. m.* 'Versicolor')

This variety has a stripy pink-and-white flower and mossy foliage.

Rosa 'Charles de Mills'

Rosa 'Charles de Mills' has double, dark crimson-purple flowers.

Rosa 'Tuscany Superb'

Another rich, dark crimson gallica, the flower of *R.* 'Tuscany Superb' is perfumed.

Rosa 'De Meaux' (syn. *R.* 'Rose de Meaux')

Hybrid musk roses

These wonderful roses give colour and perfume for almost the whole summer, as they are repeat flowering. The following varieties are ideal for hedging or informal screens.

Rosa 'Felicia'

A lovely silvery pink rose with a superb fragrance. It makes a large bushy shrub which flowers right up to the first frost.

Rosa 'Moonlight'

Rosa 'Moonlight' is a semi-double, creamy-white rose with yellow stamens and dark red stems. It has an arching habit so is better used to grow through a hedge rather than on its own.

Rosa 'Nur Mahal'

This rose has semi-double, dark red, very fragrant flowers. Its sturdy, vigorous growth lends itself to forming fragrant screens or semi-formal hedges.

Rosa 'Pax'

Like *R.* 'Moonlight', *R.* 'Pax' has a semi-double, creamy-white flower, but this one has golden stamens and dark green foliage. It is also similar in habit to *R.* 'Moonlight' and should be used in the same way.

Rosa 'Penelope'

A very beautiful, double, shell pink rose, this forms heavy trusses of flowers throughout the summer. It is similar in habit to *R.* 'Nur Mahal' so can be used in the same ways.

Centifolia (Provence) roses

The centifolia roses, often referred to as cabbage roses, were cultivated during the Middle Ages and are often mentioned in descriptions of Elizabethan and monastic gardens. They are highly perfumed and very beautiful. Several of the roses in this group are suitable for low-growing hedges, in particular, *R.* 'De Meaux'.

Rosa 'De Meaux' (syn. *R.* 'Rose de Meaux')

This is a lovely, dark pink, scented rose which responds well to tight clipping.

Polyantha roses

The polyantha group dates back to 1875 when Guillot, a French rose grower, crossed *R. multiflora* with a China rose to produce *R.* 'Ma Paquerette'. The polyanthas have large clusters of small blooms which last over a long flowering period.

Rosa 'The Fairy' (syn. *Rosa* 'Fairy Rose')

This is a low-growing, shrubby rose which only reaches about 2ft (60cm) in height. This makes it ideal for low, informal hedging or ground cover. Its tiny, pink, rounded flowers are continuous throughout the summer.

Rugosa roses

These roses make excellent dense and fast-growing hedges. They have small, bristly thorns, wrinkly leaves and beautiful, multi-petalled roses followed by large autumn hips. The hips are often used to make rosehip syrup, which is full of vitamin C.

As well as producing very vigorous hedges, these roses can also be grown as large specimen bushes.

They have a strong suckering habit so they need to be kept well pruned in order to maintain their shape. They are so vigorous that pruning can be tackled with hedging shears without fear of any unsightly damage. Pruning can also enhance the floral display of the rugosas as they produce their best flowers on new shoots.

Rosa 'Blanche Double de Coubert'

This rose has apple green foliage and large, white, semi-double flowers. It makes a loose hedge that grows to about 6 x 5ft (1.8 x 1.5m).

Rosa 'Hansa'

This strong, floriferous and fragrant rose has large, double, deep purple-crimson flowers. It has light green, large and ridged leaves and is dense in growth. Its autumn hips are plump and pointed.

Rosa 'Roseraie de l'Haÿ'

This abundant, leafy rose bears many flowers through summer to autumn. The velvety, cerise flower is heavily perfumed.

Rosa 'Fru Dagmar Hastrup'

This is a lovely rugosa rose and makes an ideal compact hedge, growing no more than 5 x 5ft (1.5 x 1.5m). It has dark green foliage and single, clear pink flowers with creamy stamens, followed by large autumn hips.

Rosa 'Schneezwerg' (syn. R. 'Snow Dwarf')

Another smaller rugosa rose, this flowers throughout the summer, producing semi-double, pure white flowers with golden stamens. It also flowers later in the season at the same time as its scarlet hips appear.

Shrub roses

These sturdy growers are relative newcomers to the rose world. Many have old-style flower formations and flower continuously throughout the summer. Quite a number of shrub roses make excellent hedges, including the following.

Rosa Heritage ('Ausblush')

This is a beautiful rose with very strongly perfumed, shell pink, cupped flowers produced on a strong, shrubby plant. It grows to around 4 x 4ft (1.2 x 1.2m).

Rosa Jacqueline du Pré ('Harwanna')

Jacqueline du Pré is a semi-double, perfumed, white rose with a healthy growth. It reaches around 4 x 3ft (1.2 x 1m).

Rosa Marjorie Fair ('Harhero')

A polyantha shrub rose, this has deep red flowers with a white eye. These are produced in clusters on fresh green foliage. This is another plant reaching 4 x 3ft (1.2 x 1m),

Rosa Westerland ('Korwest')

This variety is a cluster-flowered shrub with bright apricot flowers and dark glossy foliage. It also reaches 4 x 3ft (1.2 x 1m).

Rosa Jacqueline du Pré ('Harwanna')

Autumn colour and winter interest

FEATURES OF AUTUMN

The gentle merging of summer into autumn is always a very evocative time of year, particularly in warmer regions where the change can be more dramatic. Summer's end is heralded by the bright colours of late-flowering plants – the bright reds, yellows and oranges of heleniums, rudbeckias and crocosmias, the vibrant pinks and purples of

ABOVE *Ligustrum ovalifolium* 'Aureum' and *Cotoneaster simonsii*
LEFT *Pyracantha coccinea*

Rubus fruticosus (blackberries)

penstemons and the dusky, velvety flowers of eupatoriums. The berries of cotoneasters and pyracanthas and the rich purple fruits of elders and viburnums all add to the variety of the season.

Hedges can also contribute to this wealth of colour and artistry; in many cases they outshine the most glorious of herbaceous borders with their dramatic change of leaf colour.

Take, for instance, the brilliant rustling beech hedge which holds its dried golden leaves throughout the winter months, the dark red and orange leaves of *Acer campestre* and *Euonymus europaeus* and the yellow leaves of rugosa roses surrounding their great, pendulous bunches of juicy, orange-red hips.

WINTER INTEREST

In winter hedgerows add interest to an otherwise cold landscape. Hedges tinged with frost or laden with snow are always a beautiful sight. At the start of winter the drying leaves and autumnal colours glisten in early morning mists and shine under frosty moonlit nights as the year is dying.

The berries of the hawthorn, hollies and black bryony, the sloes of blackthorn and the greenish-yellow flowers of the ivies make a wonderful, colourful patchwork. Sloes and blackberries can be picked and enjoyed in apple and blackberry pies, crab apple jellies and sloe gin to enliven the coldest day and night as winter draws in. (See the section on cooking with wild fruits and flowers, p 130.)

75

Hedgerows also provide a nurturing winter environment that is supportive of many other plants. They may be frosted over with the dying seedpods of the wild clematis old man's beard, and the typical wet weather encourages wild mushrooms and toadstools to flourish in the damp conditions at their base. Beneath the soil, the next year's primroses and snowdrops are already beginning to stir.

EVERGREEN OR DECIDUOUS

Using deciduous shrubs for your hedge may give a bare winter boundary but their changing appearance through the seasons does make them a very interesting feature.

Conversely, the permanence of an evergreen hedge may be reassuring in its constancy of shape and density, but it will provide no added interest as the seasons change. Gardens do take on another life during winter and the hedge is part of that ever-changing environment.

EVERGREENS AND SEMI-EVERGREENS

Abelia x *grandiflora* (see p 52)
Berberis julianae (see p 53)
x *Cupressocyparis leylandii* 'Galway Gold' (syn. x *C. l.* 'Castlewellan')
Hedera helix 'Glymii' (see p 42)
Juniperus virginiana
Lonicera nitida 'Baggesen's Gold' (see p 42)
Pistacia lentiscus (see p 27)
Pyracantha spp. (see pp 57 and 99)

EVERGREENS AND SEMI-EVERGREENS

The shrubs listed below all have interest besides their evergreen properties. Some have flowers and permanent colour, with golden leaves adding autumnal interest. Many have been described in previous chapters, as listed above.

x *Cupressocyparis leylandii* 'Galway Gold' (syn. x *C. l.* 'Castlewellan')

The coniferous species, such as x *Cupressocyparis leylandii* 'Galway Gold', which turns a golden bronze-green with age, are a permanent source of autumn and winter colour. (See also pp 28 and 38.)

Juniperus virginiana
Another conifer providing good autumn and winter colour. Some plants turn a dark plum during late autumn. This species has been described more fully in the section on evergreens (see p 38).

DECIDUOUS
Non-flowering

Acer campestre
Amelanchier lamarckii
Berberis x *ottawensis* 'Superba' (syn.
    B. x *o.* 'Purpurea') (see p 53)
Berberis thunbergii (see p 53)
Carpinus betulus (see p 16)
Chaenomeles spp. (see p 54)
Cornus spp.
Cornus alba 'Sibirica'
Cornus sanguinea (see p 34)
Cornus stolonifera
Corylus avellana (see p 54)
Cotoneaster divaricatus (see p 55)
Crataegus monogyna (see p 16)
Euonymus europaeus
Fagus sylvatica
Prunus cerasifera (see p 29)
Prunus spinosa (see p 17)
Ribes alpinum (see p 32)
Sambucus nigra (see p 30)
Spiraea thunbergii (NB: this species may be
    deciduous or semi-evergreen) (see p 58)
Symphoricarpus spp. (see p 32)

DECIDUOUS
Non-flowering

Many of the trees and shrubs that are so useful for autumn colour are deciduous, losing their leaves during winter. Because of this it is important to site them carefully: if they are planted as a single-species hedge, there will be very little interest during the winter months. In cold winters, however, deciduous hedges take on a new lease of life – frost clinging to their bare branches makes them sparkle in the winter sunshine. They can also be very decorative with ivies or wild roses threading through their bare branches to create a new dimension. Remember that hedges only lose their leaves from mid-autumn to early spring so they are only bare for four months at the most and the new spring growth is always such a welcome sight.

Most of the following shrubs have been described in previous chapters, as listed left.

Acer campestre
The brilliant autumn colours of acers are well-known to nature-lovers and *Acer campestre*, a much-used 'filler' in indigenous hedges, is no exception. In autumn their rich red leaves add great splashes of colour to country hedgerows.

Acer campestre

Cornus alba 'Sibirica'

Amelanchier lamarckii

This shrub can be grown to form an upright screen or hedge. It bears lovely sprays of tiny white flowers in spring, followed by berries. The leaves turn a copper-red in autumn. *Amelanchier lamarckii* also makes a splendid small tree, if grown as a specimen, and can reach 15ft (4.5m).

Cornus spp.

Cornus species lose their leaves through the autumn, then show off their glistening, shiny stems throughout the winter. They all have wonderful autumn colour and winter interest and deserve a place in the smallest garden, if only to enjoy these qualities. When used as edging or boundaries for water areas, they come into their own during autumn and winter, but they do need to be cut back hard in the early spring to encourage this winter display.

Cornus alba 'Sibirica'

This variety is a little misleadingly named: it produces cream-and-green striped leaves but its dark red stems brighten the late autumn and winter months. They positively glow in frosty mornings and glisten when the sun shines on the cobwebs that are frequently suspended between their branches.

Cornus stolonifera

Cornus stolonifera has variegated green leaves and its golden stems continue through the winter, creating the same effect as *C. alba* 'Sibirica'.

Euonymus europaeus

This well-known, vigorous hedgerow shrub has a green stem which produces red capsules in autumn. It can also be grown as a small tree.

Fagus sylvatica (common beech)

This shrub has been described in other sections but I feel it is important to include it here as well because of its versatility. Its leaves are the most lovely light green in spring and summer, and turn copper yellow in autumn. If a beech hedge is trimmed in late summer, which is the best time to prune it, the hedge will hold its dead and dying leaves and they will rustle throughout the winter. Birds love beech as it provides some protection from the cold winds. (See also p 17.)

DECIDUOUS
Flowering

Forsythia spp. (see p 55)
Fuchsia spp. (see p 26)
Hydrangea spp.
Hydrangea macrophylla (see p 55)
Kerria japonica (see p 57)
Malus huphensis (see p 49)
Philadelphus spp. (see p 50)
Rugosa roses
Rosa virginiana (see p 69)
Spiraea thunbergii (see p 58)
Syringa spp. (see p 51)
Tamarix spp. (see p 25)
Weigela spp. (see p 58)

Flowering

The following plants are flowering, deciduous shrubs. Most have been described in previous chapters, as listed in the panel below.

Hydrangea spp.

The leaves of hydrangeas change colour gently throughout autumn until they are lost completely during the winter months. Most hydrangea leaves are pale to mid-green through the spring and summer, darkening to a deeper green as autumn approaches. Some species turn a golden bronze or dark red in cooler weather and many have a blotched but colourful appearance until they lose their leaves with the first frosts.

On most species, the veins of mature leaves also turn red or dark brown in autumn and these stand out, particularly on leaves that turn yellow.

The drying flower heads stay on throughout the winter, forming filigreed petals as they disintegrate. Ideally, these should be removed by deadheading and cut back to encourage flowering in the spring. On a large hedge this is not always practical, but it can be incorporated in regular renewal pruning in early spring.

Hydrangeas have also been described in the section on flowers and fragrance (see p 55).

Rugosa roses

Rugosa roses, particularly where they are used to grow through a mixed or indigenous hedge, improve the visual quality of the environment in autumn as well as providing a great source of winter food for wildlife, so they deserve a special mention here. Their yellow leaves last well into the winter, only dropping during really cold spells. This group has been more fully described in the section on roses (see p 72).

DESIGN

*Sculptural shapes
and uses*

Topiary, pleaching and plashing

The winding paths of a maze

TOPIARY

History

The development of topiary dates back at least 5,000 years. It was first practised, in its most basic form, by the vine growers of the Caspian region. They found that pruning back vines to the old wood encouraged new growth, flowers and fruit, so applied this method to other shrubs, and the practice of clipping hedges began. The more adventurous began to clip their hedges into specific shapes and from this, topiary grew. Shaping plants into chosen forms has been practised since Pliny the Elder in the first century AD.

LEFT Topiary 'helter-skelter' style

Records show that the Persians probably formed pleached hedges (see p 90) prior to the Greek invasion of Persia in the third century BC. During the Dark Ages, monasteries kept the skills of topiary alive. Mazes were created in monastic grounds as a tool for developing patience and persistence – in trying to find the way out. These were formed with myrtle, thyme and shrubby germander plants which were kept low growing. Later, mazes were formed with tall hedges but this low-growing form was believed to be more character-forming and to encourage self-discipline as, being low, the plants could be easily stepped over to avoid having to find the route out.

Roman gardeners were the first to use high hedges for garden ornamentation. They sculpted alcoves into hedges to house seats, statues or fountains in order to control perspective and create an attractive space for peaceful contemplation. This idea was later adopted by monasteries; in the Mediterranean, tall hedges of pittosporum, tightly clipped to encourage density, were used in monastic gardens. The use of low hedges as borders developed into a

passion for knot gardens. The ground between the hedge outline was originally filled with coloured gravel but later, with blocks of colour created by plants. In medieval herb gardens boundary hedges were kept higher than the herbs which filled their internal spaces; these were clipped very low to retain their strength of colour. The golden thymes, marjorams and silver artemisias were firm favourites in the old herb gardens as they responded well to vigorous clipping. Cloister herb gardens often had neat geometric beds intersected with pathways for ease of harvesting and maintenance.

In time these knot gardens developed into more adventurous shapes. The hedges were allowed to grow much higher and tunnels and arches were formed from the hedging plants. Yew was particularly popular used in this way. Soon more imaginative shapes were created – balls, pyramids and spirals as well as animals and birds. Box and yew became synonymous with topiary as their growth pattern and response to close clipping was particularly suitable for this type of work. Double box borders with small trees – often in topiary

Low hedge borders highlight the colours of the bedding plants

Part of the knot garden at Barnsley House (Gloucestershire, England)

shapes – set at their apices became popular, and were used to enclose both herbs and roses. In Italy this style was often used in formal gardens, particularly during the seventeenth century when terraced Renaissance gardens were at their peak. In seventeenth-century England John Tradescant the Elder, a great gardener and botantist, created walkways and topiary shapes from yew while in France, André Le Nôtre became famous for his parterre gardens, examples of which can be seen at Vaux-le-Vicomte and Versailles. In England there are wonderful examples of knot gardens at Hever Castle, while Rosemary Verey's beautiful garden at Barnsley House boasts a very pretty knot design laid out on a gravel bed. Christopher Lloyd's garden at Great Dixter has majestic shapes clipped from

Christopher Lloyd's topiary shapes at Great Dixter (East Sussex, England)

André Le Nôtre

André Le Nôtre was one of the greatest garden designers of the seventeenth century. After first studying art and architecture, he began his gardening career in 1635 at the age of 22 when he became gardener for Gaston d' Orléans, brother of King Louis XIII, at the Jardins du Luxembourg. In 1637 he was promoted to Head Gardener of the Tuileries in Paris. The intricate garden he created at Vaux-le-Vicomte, between 1656 and 1661, made his name. For this he was commissioned by Nicholas Fouquet, First Minister of Finance in the Court of King Louis XIV (the Sun King). Louis XIV, jealous of Fourquet, imprisoned him on the grounds of treason and Le Nôtre and his team of gardeners were employed by the King to create a garden at Versailles, beginning in 1661. Le Nôtre had begun designing parterre gardens in the 1640s and many of his designs, by this time, had been incorporated into the King's gardens.

Many of the gardens that Le Nôtre designed still exist today, including those at Chantilly, Saint-Cloud, Sceaux and Marly. His influence filtered right around Europe and many gardeners embraced his French 'formal' style.

When the 'natural landscape' style of Lancelot 'Capability' Brown, developed in England, started to influence garden design in Europe in the late eighteenth century, Le Nôtre's formal style came to be regarded with some disdain by the more 'naturalistic' designers. By the second half of the eighteenth century, topiary had dropped out of fashion and was thought to be in bad taste. Le Nôtre's use of carpet bedding and low-growing box parterre gardens was considered too contrived but a revival of his style sprang up in the early twentieth century when Dubois, Head Gardener of the Tuileries, laid out a new garden at Jardin du Carousel, in front of the Louvre, in this style. The French received this garden, echoing the time of the Sun King, enthusiastically. Nowadays, the renewed interest in box hedging and its use for parterres and as edging for potagers and herb gardens is helping to keep the spirit of André Le Nôtre alive.

the yew. In Italy the magnificent Villa Gamberaia at Settignano, just outside Florence, has an idyllic parterre and water garden set high in the hills.

It is interesting to note that after Henry VIII's dissolution of the monastries – around 1530 – many monastic gardens were taken over by the lay gardeners who had been tending them and cultivation for commercial purposes began. The birth of the garden industry can be attributed to this era. Many of these early 'nurseries' would have grown hedging plants and supplied them to the great gardens of England for use in their elaborate mazes and labyrinths.

William Barron and Elvaston Castle

There was one garden begun in the early nineteenth century that took topiary and hedging to its heart. In 1829 the Fourth Earl of Harrington, owner of the neogothic Elvaston Castle in Derby, married his mistress, the actress Maria Foote, causing a scandal in society. In order to make his home a beautiful, reclusive retreat, far from the wagging tongues of London society, the Earl appointed a talented young Scottish gardener, William Barron. His brief was to create the most lavish garden imaginable within the castle grounds.

William Barron had a love of evergreen shrubs and trees. Much of his design was based around established topiary and large evergreen trees which he persuaded the Earl to allow him to purchase and have moved to the site at Elvaston. His golden yews became famous and by 1849 the gardens boasted more than 1,000 of them. Around 1850, miles of clipped evergreen hedges were recorded along with amazing topiary and exotic trees. Green and golden yews were used alternately to form a large hedge around a monkey puzzle tree (Araucaria araucana) which, in turn, was surrounded by alternately planted golden holly and common yew, tightly clipped to a height of 9ft (3m). In the 'Alhambra Garden' – just one of the imaginative gardens within the grounds – low scrolls and swirls of clipped golden yew were laid out along pathways of octagonal bricks. Bedding plants, including senecio, cineraria, lobelia and pelargonium, added colour to the hedges, which were also punctuated with glorious topiary and statues.

The Earl died suddenly in 1851. As he had no heir, his four-year-old son having died in 1836, the castle passed on to his brother, Leicester Stanhope. Unfortunately, he did not have sufficient wealth to keep the gardens up to their high standard. William Barron's staff was drastically reduced and the grounds were opened to a paying public in order to assist with their upkeep. The gardens slowly declined through lack of maintenance. The mature shrubs that had been brought in to the site were planted very closely together for effect, and these began to battle with each other for light. Dieback, lack of care and meagre bedding displays between the parterre and hedged areas soon gave the garden an unkempt appearance.

Finally, after a sad history of neglect, the castle contents and garden statues were auctioned in 1964. A consortium formed by Derbyshire Borough and County Council bought the site and they turned it into the first of England's Country Parks.

However, its future is still uncertain and until such time as a decision is made about the castle's use, its golden yews, its clipped hedges and some of its magnificent topiary can still be seen there.

IDEAL PLANTS FOR TOPIARY

Buxus spp. (see p 40)

Ilex spp. (see p 29)

Ilex aquifolium 'J.C. van Tol'

Ilex crenata

Laurus nobilis (see p 44)

Taxus baccata (see p 39)

IDEAL PLANTS FOR TOPIARY

Topiary is a contrived form of decoration and while it is very well suited to formal and classical styles of gardening, and can add an interesting touch to many informal gardens, it does look somewhat out of place in more naturalistic settings and in wilder, cottage-style gardens.

The most commonly used plants for topiary are listed above. For deciduous hedges and pleaching use lime, hornbeam and beech.

Ilex aquifolium 'J.C. van Tol'

This self-pollinating holly is very popular as berries will form on the clipped shape adding an ornamental interest.

Ilex crenata (box-leaved holly, Japanese holly)

Ilex crenata, a narrow-leafed and much slower-growing species, is also very good for topiary.

Topiary today

Where to see topiary in England

Barnsley House, Barnsley, Gloucestershire

Great Dixter, Northiam, East Sussex

Hampton Court Palace, Kingston, Surrey

Hever Castle, Hever, Kent

Penshurst Place, Penshurst, Kent

Physic Garden, Chelsea, London

The Courts Garden, Trowbridge, Wiltshire

Ilex aquifolium 'J. C. van Tol'

WILL RESPOND TO TRAINING

Berberis darwinii (see p 52)

Hebe rakaiensis (see p 27)

Hedera helix 'Glymii' (see p 42)

Ligustrum ovalifolium (see p 44)

Lonicera nitidia (see p 42)

Olearia nummulariifolia

Osmanthus heterophyllus (see p 42)

Santolina chamaecyparissus (see p 60)

The following plants also respond well to clipping and have pliable growth suitable for training.

Olearia nummulariifolia

I have not included *Olearia nummulariifolia* in any of the previous chapters because it is usually grown as a specimen shrub. It is one of the hardiest of the olearias and has an abundance of thick, pale green leaves which are borne on crowded stems. It will produce insignificantly small but fragrant flowers if left to grow naturally but its dense habit makes it a good specimen for shaping and the constant clipping required for topiary would probably not allow it to flower.

In practice

The only tools required for topiary are pruning shears, sharp secateurs, bamboo cane and garden string. Templates aren't essential, but they will help you create whatever shape you want. They can be purchased from good garden centres. The plants listed above can all be persuaded to grow around these templates and are dense enough in habit to respond well to tight clipping.

The main secret of topiary is to prune little and often and plants to be shaped must be young enough that they will respond to this treatment. For this type of work plants can be grown very

Olearia nummulariifolia

successfully in pots and the more simple shapes – including balls and cones – can be pruned and clipped freehand. If you buy a plant that has already been trained into a shape, the same rules apply. Remember that, as for pruning any evergreen hedge, they should not be clipped after late summer as this may lead to frost damage on the new growth.

Topiary balls and cones, particularly if grown in pots, do give the garden a sense of formality and style; they can be placed in strategic positions to give just the right effect.

Training topiary requires patience and a steady hand. The plant can either be planted directly in its position in the ground or in a container. Position the template or former over the plant. Originally, these were made from wood so that they rotted

A selection of metal topiary frames

away by the time the shape reached maturity. Nowadays, strip metal or heavy gauge wire is used. Wire mesh formers, which can be bought from any good garden centres, are often used for the more elaborate shapes, such as birds and animals.

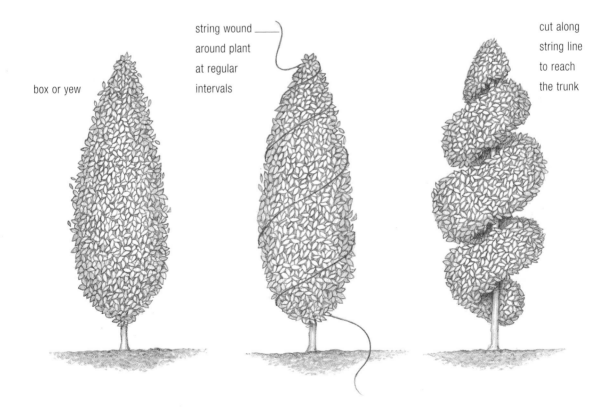

box or yew

string wound around plant at regular intervals

cut along string line to reach the trunk

Cutting a spiral shape

As the new, flexible stems grow, train them around the former by weaving them in and around the mesh or wires. Once the frame is covered, clip new growth back against the shape regularly.

To make a spiral shape, wind a piece of string around a conical-shaped shrub, in a spiral; *Buxus* spp. or *Taxus baccata* are the best for this purpose as they have very small leaves. Cut a shallow channel where the string lies. Once the channel is clearly defined, remove the string and clip deeper into it until you reach the trunk. The remaining foliage can be clipped tightly to round off the overall shape. Always use small, sharp hedging or sheep shears, or scissors if the plant is particularly small.

PLEACHING

Pleaching makes a hedge on stilts. The term 'pleaching' comes from the French verb *plessier*, to plait, and this is exactly how a pleached hedge or

screen looks. Lime and hornbeam are particularly suitable for this purpose; they can form a lovely, intertwining hedge to line a path or even an avenue. This gives a very formal edging and is quite majestic when fully grown. While hornbeams and limes give the best effect, maples and sycamores can also be used for this purpose.

A pleached hornbeam avenue

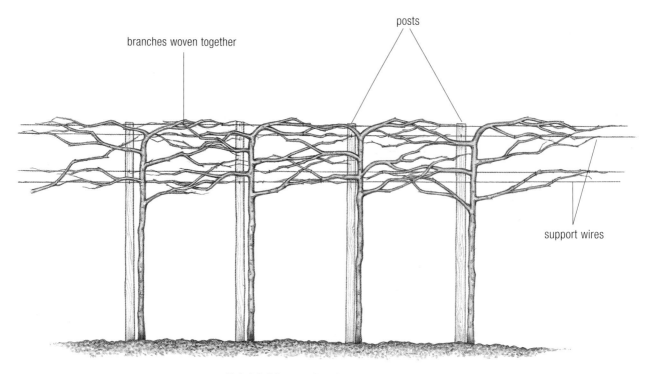

Establishing a pleached hedge

In practice

To establish a pleached hedge, plant the trees at regular intervals along the line of the path or edge. Allow them to grow to the height required but keep the bottom of the trunks – around 5ft (1.5m) – bare. At either end, and alongside each tree, drive a support stake into the ground. Stretch wires between these supports at the level of the first branches to be pleached, and then at regular intervals of around 2ft (60cm) until you reach the required height of the hedge. As the branches grow, cut and weave them together laterally to form a plait or woven screen; the idea is to prevent the branches from growing vertically.

Once the pleached screen is established, clip it as with any hedge, making sure that any stray vertical branches are encouraged to grow laterally.

PLASHING

Plashing, or laying, is the old country method of hedge cutting, and is used to make an impenetrable hedgerow between fields and alongside lanes.

Traditional hedge laying, using chestnut supports

In practice

To develop a plashed hedge, cut into the established trunks of the shrubs so that they bend forwards, and weave the branches together. Drive support posts into the ground at regular intervals – chestnut is the usual material – and plait the top branches neatly together, around the posts. Any new branches will grow vertically from the lateral branches to form a dense hedge. To maintain it, clip in late summer – this is usually done with a mechanical hedge cutter – and lay it again in early spring, before the new growth begins.

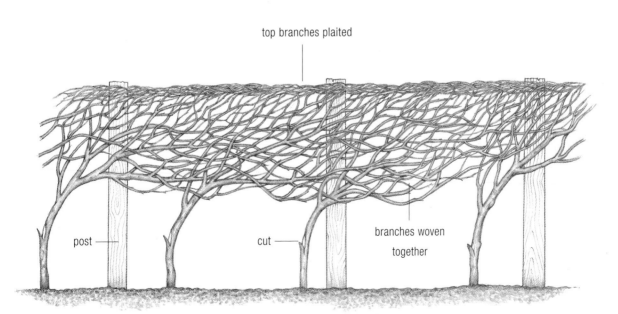

top branches plaited

post — | cut — | branches woven together

Establishing a plashed hedge

Screens and boundaries

SEPARATING DIFFERENT AREAS IN A GARDEN

For separating different areas of the garden, yew, box and privet work extremely well as clipped formal hedges. Box can divide flower beds or provide edges to paths as in old-fashioned parterre gardens, whilst yew and privet can be clipped into more distinctive shapes. (For more detailed information on this subject, see p 88.)

One of the most well-known gardens to separate areas with hedges is Sissinghurst Castle in Kent. Here the famous writer and gardener Vita Sackville-West and her husband Harold Nicolson separated the garden into 'rooms' using box and

ABOVE Box edging in the gardens at Sissinghurst Castle

LEFT Lavender edging beside a garden path

Clematis montana 'Pink Perfection' trained to grow over tree and fence

yew hedges. The yew hedges were allowed to grow very tall to form the geometric outline of the garden. Box was used, particularly in the famous white garden, to compartmentalize the beautiful selection of white herbaceous plants, bulbs and roses. Laid out in a series of rectangles, the box hedges – 2–3ft (60–100cm) in height – surround the different planting areas.

Garden rooms have become a popular feature again in recent years. Any number of the hedging plants described in other chapters of this book can be used to fulfil this function. With imagination and some daring, a garden can be laid out to personalize one's own space. Yew and box tend to formalize a garden, but I have used a low, variegated box hedge to surround a very small hot bed and this worked extremely well in an otherwise informal cottage atmosphere. (A hot bed is a herbaceous bed of rich reds, vibrant yellows and oranges. They are always planted in full sun and flower in high summer.)

SCREENING UNSIGHTLY AREAS

A tank or trellis separating compost and work areas in the garden can easily be concealed by a *Clematis montana*, of which there are numerous beautiful varieties. The most rampant include *C. m.* var. *rubens* 'Tetrarose', a lovely pink as its name suggests, and *C. m. alba*, a vigorous white subspecies. Clematis require very little maintenance. One of mine, a *C. m.* var. *rubens*, completely hides my oil tank and is a picture from mid-spring to early summer, some years even into midsummer. All I do is cut out the over-vigorous areas with secateurs when necessary. Strictly, *C. montana* cannot be regarded as a hedging plant, but once established on a man-made screen or object, they become so thick that the description 'hedge' is the most suitable one. Any of the climbing clematis species can be used to grow through or into a hedge and those that do not need to be cut hard to the ground in early spring are the most useful.

Polygonum baldschuanicum, also known as mile-a-minute plant and Russian vine, is a rampant climber with long shoots sporting heart-shaped flowers. Towards the end of summer, tiny frothy white flowers burst forth, sweetly fragrant. This climber is often used to disguise ugly walls, sheds or dead tree stumps but can be used to scramble through an old hedge just as effectively, clothing it with creamy white flowers at the start of autumn. However, it is deciduous and does need judicious pruning to keep it within bounds.

Symphoricarpos can produce a good screening effect with its pretty pink buds which burst into glistening white berries in early autumn. This plant does have a suckering habit though so it should be restrained with careful pruning. Although it is classed as a deciduous shrub, the berries last well into winter and it will at least disguise an ugly screen even if it does not completely hide it during winter.

The brilliant white fruits of the snowberry (*Symphoricarpos albus*) hang in massed clumps

TALL HEDGES

x *Cupressocyparis leylandii* (see p 28)
Prunus laurocerasus (see p 45)
Prunus lusitanica (see p 30)
Taxus baccata (see pp 31 and 39)
Viburnum tinus (see p 51)

TALL HEDGES

Tall hedges are particularly useful for screening areas in the garden that are ugly or being used for other purposes, such as housing an oil tank, a garden shed or a compost heap. They can also make good screens or boundary lines for vegetable patches, though you must take care siting a hedge for this purpose; make sure that it will not take away too much light from the vegetable garden and that the roots of the hedge will not extend into the growing area. I have screened a vegetable area with a laurel hedge, *Prunus laurocerasus*, and it looked beautiful. The growing area for the vegetables was laid out at a considerable distance from the hedge boundary and was in an open, southerly position.

Areas at the foot of tall hedges do become very arid, as the roots of the hedge rob the soil of nutrients and moisture so that little else will grow. However, this is not a problem when using tall hedges purely as screening and for this purpose, evergreen hedges are the most desirable. *Viburnum tinus,* with its lovely pink-white flowers in late winter/early spring and glossy green leaves throughout the year, makes a very good screen requiring little pruning – just enough to keep the hedge in shape. *Prunus laurocerasus* is another ideal solution for ugly areas, as long as you have enough space: they grow both wide and tall. Hedges of both plants need sufficient space around them to flourish.

A tall screen of shaped evergreens

TALL AND NARROW

Carpinus betulus (see p 16)

Cotoneaster simonsii (see p 55)

Fagus sylvatica (see p 17)

Prunus cerasifera (see p 29)

Prunus cerasifera 'Pissardii' (see p 30)

TALL AND NARROW

For smaller, tighter areas, *Cotoneaster simonsii* will reach 10–12ft (3–3.5m) in height but only 1ft (30cm) or so in width. *Prunus cerasifera*, beech and hornbeams are also suitable for narrower areas though they are deciduous. *Fagus sylvatica* (beech) and *Carpinus betulus* (hornbeam), although technically described as deciduous, do hold their dying leaves through the winter, shedding them fully only when new growth starts in the spring.

Tall hedges can also be used decoratively within the garden. They can act as a shelter or provide a screen for seating areas. Admittedly, only a larger garden is really suitable for this treatment but a tightly clipped yew or beech, planted in a semi-circle or other curved shape within the available space, can look very attractive with seating arranged to fit it and planted tubs or urns arranged to highlight its shape.

LOW HEDGES

Berberis spp. (see p 52)

Fuchsia spp. (see p 26)

Genista hispanica (see p 23)

Rosa spp. (see pp 64–73)

Spiraea spp. (see p 58)

LOW HEDGES

Low hedges can be used in gardens where views of the surrounding countryside are an important feature but where a garden boundary is necessary. For instance, a country garden with surrounding views could be edged with fuchsias, *Genista hispanica* (Spanish gorse), berberis, spiraeas or roses to give the garden an informal and colourful edge

without marking the boundary in a harsh way. As an alternative, an indigenous hedge could be the answer or, if a more regular evergreen hedge is used, clematis can be grown through it. All of these plants would make lovely low hedges if kept clipped to the desired height.

Fuchsia magellanica as a hedge

A very colourful hedge of *Genista hispanica* (Spanish gorse)

TOWN GARDENS

Carpinus betulus (see p 16)

Ceanothus spp. (see p 54)

Cistus spp. (see p 32)

Cotoneaster spp. (see p 54)

Fagus sylvatica (see p 17)

Forsythia spp. (see p 55)

Fuchsia spp. (see p 26)

Ilex aquifolium (see p 29)

Ligustrum spp. (see p 44)

Lonicera nitida (see p 42)

Olearia x *haastii* (see p 23)

Spiraea spp. (see p 58)

Viburnum tinus (see p 51)

Weigela spp. (see p 58)

TOWN GARDENS

Hedging for town gardens is very much up to the individual's requirements – most hedge plants will grow as well in the town as in the country. Obviously the need for plants that are resistant to pollution is a consideration depending upon where one lives. Suburban gardens tend not to suffer as much pollution as inner city gardens. The width and height of hedge required must also be taken into consideration.

Colourful hedges can break up the masses of brick, concrete, and tarmac. Some flowering hedges – spiraea, weigela and, for early spring, forsythia – are particularly good for this purpose. If evergreen screens are required *Viburnum tinus,* with its pretty flowers, is excellent, provided the space available is not too small. The compact *Olearia* x *haastii,* with its daisy-like flowers, also does well in the town.

If the area is particularly subject to pollution, and it is formal hedging that you require, beech (including the purple beech, *Fagus sylvatica* f. *purpurea*), cotoneaster, pyracantha, holly, hornbeam, privet and lonicera will all cope. For flowering or coloured hedges a popular town plant is the hydrangea which can be used more as a screen than a formal hedge. One of the advantages of town gardens is that they are often more sheltered than country gardens, so in many areas some of the more tender plants can be used, including fuchsia, ceanothus and cistus. The list of hedging plants for coastal areas could be used as a basis for choice in the more southern towns of England (see p 20).

Visit the local park or other planted areas – main roads or areas around office blocks – to see what plants have been used there. This will give you some ideas about what will flourish locally and allow you to see how they look in an urban setting. Bear in mind the size and aspects of your space; what encloses the garden, does it get early morning or afternoon sun, is it windy? Consider also the width of paths and the proximity of pavements so as not to encroach. Brickwork and paving, used imaginatively, can make the smallest of gardens beautiful and interesting havens of tranquility.

This colourful hedge breaks up the areas of brick in the buildings and along the drive

A colourful spring hedge of forsythia and *Ribes sanguinea*

AS A DETERRENT

Berberis darwinii

Berberis x *ottawensis* 'Superba'

Berberis x *stenophylla* (see p 53)

Chaenomeles cathayensis

Crataegus monogyna (see p 16)

Hippophae rhamnoides (see p 23)

Ilex aquifolium

Mahonia aquifolium

Prunus cerasifera (see p 29)

Pyracantha coccinea

Rugosa roses (see p 72)

AS A DETERRENT

Where a hedge or boundary is required for protection or to stop animals from either leaving or entering an area, the following shrubs will form a thick, impenetrable hedge. They all produce thorns which not only knit the hedge closely together but are a deterrent to humans and animals alike.

Berberis darwinii

For small, low-growing hedges to deter cats or smaller animals, *Berberis darwinii* is a good choice. It makes a thick, prickly hedge, will give year-round colour in suburban gardens, and, if kept well clipped, gives a neat, tidy edge to any garden. This species has also been described in the section on flowers and fragrance (see p 52).

Chaenomeles cathayensis

This is a particularly thorny species and will form a very prickly hedge if it is clipped back hard in the spring. Its flowers are not as luscious as some of the other species, such as the dark red *C.* x *superba* 'Boule de Feu', but it does produce much larger, rich green fruits in the autumn and would make a very interesting hedge for an urban garden. I have seen *C. japonica* used to frame a very small cottage garden and the rich red flowers against mellow brick is truly picturesque. This species has also been described in the section on flowers and fragrance (see p 54).

Ilex aquifolium

This plant also has extremely deterrent qualities. However, hollies generally are fairly slow growing and so are not very practical if a secure boundary hedge is needed quickly. They do make lovely thick, glossy hedges but more than a little patience

is required. Mixed in with hawthorn or blackthorn, they add to its impenetrability and enliven an otherwise rather dull hedge in winter. This species has also been described in the section on windy sites (see p 29).

Mahonia aquifolium

Mahonia aquifolium, with its dense, suckering habit and slightly prickly, spiny leaves, also makes a good deterrent hedge. It has the added bonus of small golden flowers and evergreen leaves which take on autumn tints. This species has also been described in the section on flowers and fragrance (see p 48).

Pyracantha coccinea

This pyracantha is particularly thorny. Once established, it produces a thick hedge and its flowers and berries increase with the regular pruning required to keep it tight. The autumn colour of both the leaves and berries is an added bonus.

Pyracantha used as a deterrent town hedge

UNUSUAL COMBINATIONS
Cottage and country gardens

To surround a cottage garden, plant a hedge of *Chaenomeles japonica* with *Viburnun tinus* at either end or running into it.

Fagus sylvatica f. *purpurea* (copper beech) and the ordinary green beech, *Fagus sylvatica,* make a wonderful combination planted alternately in blocks to give a chequerboard effect.

Hollies with ivies scrambling over them and entwined in their branches is a lovely countryside combination. Both are evergreen. In spring, the fresh new leaves of the ivy add a new dimension to the hedge and in autumn, the ivy flowers are sprinkled through the hedge like tiny lanterns. Take care not to let the ivy get the upper hand; clipped like any other hedging shrub, the ivy will retain its glossy appearance.

Rosa eglanteria (sweet briar) and *R. rugosa* varieties can also be a good host for the vigorous *Clematis montana*. Clipping to keep the hedges in trim will encourage the growth of the clematis without reducing its vigour. The pretty *Clematis montana* var. *rubens* 'Marjorie', a variety with a lovely, small, softly striped pink flowers and rather grey-green leaves, looks beautiful intertwining with the sturdy rose branches, and it flowers from late spring to early summer, before the roses show their glory. *Clematis montana* var. *rubens* 'Tetrarose' and *C. m.* var. *r.* 'Superba' *(syn. C. m.* 'Rubens Superba') are also suitable for this treatment.

Lonicera periclymenum (honeysuckle) is another natural hedging climber which blends well, particularly in the less formal indigenous hedges, adding colour and fragrance.

Coastal gardens

In coastal areas, where less hardy hedging plants thrive, *Fuchsia magellanica* growing amongst *Olearia* x *haastii* or *O. macrodonta* is a pleasing combination in summer. The loose, arching branches of the fuchsia and its dark red, pendulous flowers are thrown into contrast against the grey-green leaves of the olearia, with its masses of cream flowers. I have seen *Hydrangea macrophylla,* in all its colours, tucked into the edge of these hedges to punctuate the hedge line. Its full, light green leaves and showy flowers blend in with the more delicate habit of fuchsia and olearia, and the overall effect is a riot of softly muted colour.

TRADITIONAL COMBINATIONS

For more formal, traditional combinations, use yew or chamaecyparis tightly clipped as a backdrop to low-clipped box, or a melange of *Buxus sempervirens* (common box) with *B. s.* 'Variegata' (a variegated cultivar). Lavenders can be mixed together to give a less formal edge to a potager or herb garden. *Lavandula angustifolia* 'Munstead' or *L. a.* 'Hidcote' (syn. *L.* 'Hidcote Blue') alternated with *L. a.* 'Rosea' (syn. *L.* 'Rosea') or *L.* 'Alba' are very delicate combinations which work well in both herb and rose gardens.

Sophora davidii

The well-known horticulturist Roy Lancaster described the unusual shrub *Sophora davidii* in an interesting article published in the May 2000 issue of *The Garden* – the Royal Horticultural Society's monthly bible. This is a deciduous shrub with attractive, fern-like leaves growing in pairs along its spine. It produces pea-like, blue-grey flowers on the previous season's growth. It is tough and hardy. In China, from where it originates, it is often used to form a hedge to keep poultry and livestock contained or to protect a vegetable garden. Although hardy and now acclimatized to our European cold, it does like a well-drained, sunny site, which will encourage it to flower. However, it is not fussy about soil and will tolerate both acid and alkaline loams. Pruning is simple too; it does not need regular clipping but old and dead wood should be thinned out from the mass of tangled branches it produces. In the right spot *S. davidii* could make a lovely hedge and provide an interesting talking point.

Sophora davidii was first discovered and introduced to the western hemisphere by Père Armand David (1826–1900), a French missionary known to most by the moniker Father David. He was also responsible for introducing the beautiful evergreen *Clematis armandii, Acer davidii,* and *Davidia involucrata* (the handkerchief tree) to our gardens.

MAINTENANCE

Keeping your hedge looking good

Preparation and planting

BUYING PLANTS

However frustrating this may seem, the smallest shrubs are the best and cheapest to buy. They will become established quickly provided, of course, that you have prepared the soil properly (see p 108) and they are easier to move if, by chance, you have made a mistake with their positioning. When purchasing small hedging plants, be sure to check that their root system is a strong one. They should have bushy, fibrous roots that form a good root ball. Most hedging plants are purchased 'bare root' during late autumn, having been newly lifted from open ground. Provided that the root systems do not dry out, they can survive out of the ground for several weeks. If you have bought a large number of hedging plants from a nursery, whether in person or by mail order, make sure that you soak the roots in water immediately on receiving them so that they become thoroughly wet. If you are not ready to plant them out, heel them into open ground in the garden until you are ready to do so. 'Heeling in' plants means digging a hole large enough to take the root balls of a group of plants, placing all the plants in this hole, and covering them with soil. By planting en masse like this, the plants will not suffer much loss of moisture while waiting to be planted in their final position.

Deciduous bare-root hedging plants are lifted once they become dormant, which is usually after the first frosts of autumn. They can be planted out at

Hoeing around young hedging plants

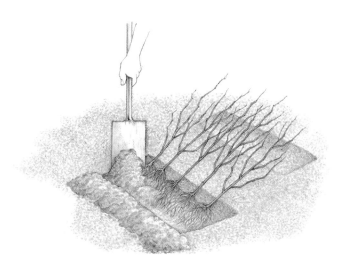

Heeling in plants

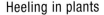

any time during the winter months provided that the ground is not frozen. This allows the plants to get their feet down into the ground before the growing season starts in early spring. Planting during late spring and summer is not advisable and a good nursery will not sell you bare-root plants during this time. Bare-root plants need plenty of moisture to establish a good root system, and hot spells – or time away during holidays – may interfere with this. You should even avoid planting container hedging plants during the summer months as they also need plenty of moisture to develop well-established roots.

Some hedging plants are not suitable for lifting bare root and so are grown in a container. Theoretically, these can be planted at any time of year, but I would not advise planting a hedge during hot weather for the reasons given above. My advice is to buy your plants in mid- or late autumn and plant them as soon as possible. Following this, it is essential to plan your hedge during the summer months and prepare the ground early in the autumn, ready to take your purchases.

Look out for the differing price structures when buying hedging plants. They are usually sold by the 10s or 100s, depending on the type, and usually, the more you buy, the cheaper they are. Buy from a reputable garden centre or nurseryman who can tell you the origin of the plants. Good root systems are developed by regular transplanting and many good forestry and tree nurserymen now supply hedging plants grown in this traditional way. Always make sure that the plants are moist when you receive them so you know that, even if they have been lifted for some time, their root systems have been kept covered. The majority of hedging plants are deciduous so dry and crinkly leaves are to be expected.

Finally, when buying suckering plants such as syringas or rhododendrons, it is important to purchase only plants that have been grown on their own roots: if they have been grafted, the suckers they produce may be of a different colour or species, which will spoil the overall effect of your hedge. Roses are generally budded onto a uniform root stock, so any resulting suckers can be seen and pulled off easily.

CHOOSING THE SITE

It is important to plan the siting of the hedge carefully. You must allow for the fact that the narrowest of hedges is going to thicken to a width of at least 18in (45cm) and in some cases could take up as much space as 36in (90mm), and bear this in mind when choosing your plants. Once established, a hedge cannot easily be moved, unlike a specimen shrub which can be dug up and replanted in a more appropriate spot if required. Remember also that the roots will spread some distance beyond the confines of the hedge and, because of the volume of the root system, the soil in much of the surrounding area will be robbed of moisture and nutrients. Other factors to consider are whether the hedge will be on a slope or in an exposed position, and what type of soil it will be growing in.

Points to remember

• Allow enough room for the hedge to grow widthways and for the roots to spread beneath the soil – never plant a hedge right up against a fence or wall

• Plant a hedge no closer to a path than 2ft (60cm). This will ensure that your hedge does not overhang or obstruct the path when fully grown

• Informal flowering hedges need more room because the clipping required is invariably less severe

From a visual point of view, consider whether a flower border is required along the length of the hedge, bearing in mind the preceding factors. Hedges often look much more attractive if hard landscaping or lawn is continued right up to their base, and if the hedge is a flowering one, the beauty of its flowers and foliage should not be detracted from. Hedges that flower from summer to autumn have a particularly long-lasting beauty. Spring-flowering hedges can be treated differently as their flowers are often over long before a summer-flowering border is in full swing.

PLANTING DISTANCES

This varies according to the size and type of plant, but as hedging plants are normally bought when they are quite small, due to the cost of purchasing large numbers of plants, the rule of thumb is that small shrubs be planted from 1–2ft (30–60cm) apart, depending on the species.

Planting in a staggered, double row

Where a deep windbreak, and therefore a really thick hedge, is required, you will need a double row; set each plant 12–18in (30–45cm) apart, and stagger them between the rows.

For single rows, 12–24in (30–60cm) apart is quite sufficient. Single-row hedges usually give a better result: the plants have plenty of space around them, both above and below ground, to grow strongly. Single-row planting is always the best method for flowering hedges, particularly of single species.

SOIL PREPARATION

The more care you put into the preparation of your soil, the better your hedge will grow. The three most important provisions in cultivating a healthy hedge are:

- sufficient space
- good drainage
- nutrient source

Sufficient space

Your first job, after deciding exactly where your hedge is to be planted, is to mark out the area with pegs and string, to the exact length and shape of the desired hedge. Next, dig a trench. Generally, this should be twice the width of the root ball and one-and-a-half times the depth. With bare-root plants this is easy to determine, but with container-grown plants it is more difficult. In this case, tip the plant out of its pot, gently unwind the root ball and tease out the fibrous roots so that you can judge the width and depth of trench the plant will need.

However, preparation does depend on the quality of your soil.

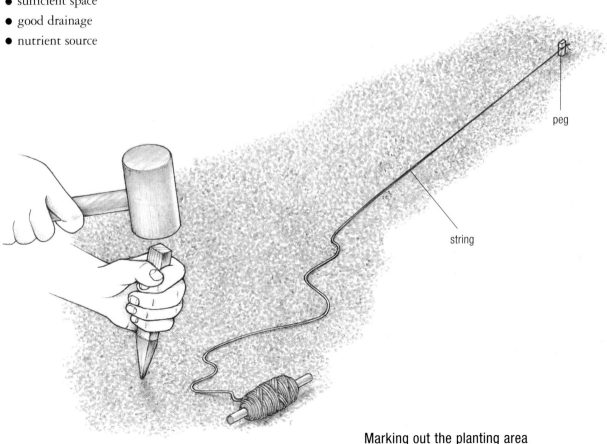

peg

string

Marking out the planting area

Good drainage

If the soil is very heavy, clay for example, it is necessary to make it more friable and improve the drainage. Very few hedging plants like sitting in water. If the trench is double dug and the soil broken up as you go, sharp sand and/or gravel can be incorporated into it to help improve its quality. If your soil is good-quality loam, friable and well drained, then a good-sized trench is sufficient. Fill in the trench loosely and you are ready for planting.

Nutrient source

If the soil is very light and sandy, then it is well worth incorporating a good layer of well-composted manure in the bottom of the trench so that the roots have a good base from which to draw food. This is particularly important for yew hedges as they are very greedy feeders, especially when establishing their root system. Do not use freshly composted materials: these can burn the young roots. Any green manure can be used as long as it has had time to decompose thoroughly. For very light soils, well-composted manure can be added to the backfill (the soil you have taken out of the trench). I always mix in a few handfuls of bonemeal when returning backfill to the trench: bonemeal is a slow-release fertilizer which will gently feed the roots throughout the winter while they are getting their feet down.

PLANTING

Planting out, I always feel, is the most exciting part. It is a very simple, easy process and, if you start in an orderly, organized manner, it does not take long. First of all, make sure your bare-root plants have been thoroughly soaked.

soil dug from first section is set aside to fill final section

soil dug from subsequent sections is used to fill section in front

Double digging

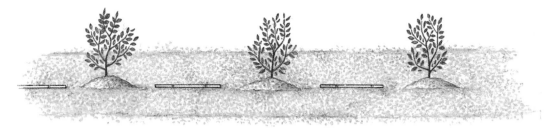

Using a cane to measure planting distances

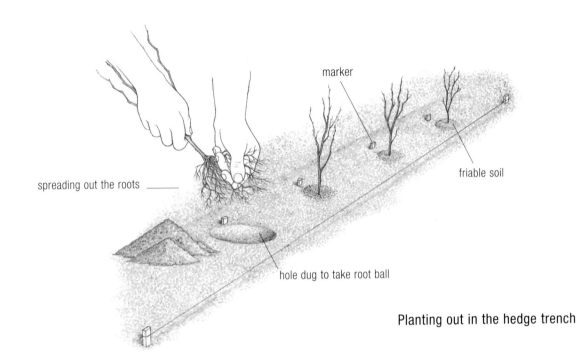

spreading out the roots

marker

friable soil

hole dug to take root ball

Planting out in the hedge trench

Your trench should now be well dug and ready to receive your plants. Either indicate the position of each planting hole with a marker or, the easiest way I think, cut a cane to the distance you want between each plant and use this to determine where to dig. Remember to start the run halfway down the stick. For example, if you are planting 18in (45cm) apart, set your first shrub 9in (22cm) in from the end of the row. Theoretically, your last plant should be 9in (22cm) from the far end. For each plant, dig out a hole deep and wide enough to take the root ball comfortably, spreading the roots out well. Backfill the hole to just above the stock of the plant, then sprinkle friable soil generously around the base of the plant, firming gently as you go to remove any air pockets in the soil around the roots. Continue along the trench until all the plants are bedded in well. Sprinkle a generous handful of bonemeal around the base of each and rake it in gently. Finally, a good watering of the hedge line will ensure that all the freshly dug earth settles down. Freshly dug earth and carefully planted shrubs always give me a great deal of satisfaction.

Now you must keep an eye on your plants. The fresh and newly fertilized earth will encourage weeds; keep them at bay or they will choke the young plants. Do not let your plants dry out.

Pruning

TOOLS

The following are the most commonly used tools for pruning and can be bought at any good garden centre or hardware store. As with most things in life, the more you pay the better quality you get. It is always worth buying good tools if you intend carrying out pruning yourself, and for a long time. It is also important to remember that shears, secateurs and knives need regular sharpening, especially if they are in constant use. Keep all cutting blades sharp and clean them after use with an oily rag to keep all the movable parts well lubricated.

ABOVE Clipping a tall hedge mechanically

LEFT Pruning buddleja by hand

Find a good, sturdy stepladder with extra legs for support if necessary. This type of ladder is particularly useful if you have high hedges to clip. There is also a 'ladder stabilizer' available; this is a strong, safe support to stop ladders toppling over or slipping sideways. For really large and long hedges a wheeled platform could be a good investment. These are adjustable so the platform can be secured at different heights. They are safe and very sturdy.

Choosing appropriate tools

Hedges that have small leaves and twiggy growth can be clipped with shears or electric/petrol-driven hedge cutters. This makes hedge maintenance much easier as it is so much faster to prune in this manner than by hand, with secateurs.

Hand pruning is usually used for very woody, branching plants with many large leaves, such as laurel, viburnum and *Acer campestre*. If electric or

Mechanical shears can snag branches and tear leaves

mechanical shears are used on these, the branches can get snagged and the leaves sliced through, leaving raw and ugly scars. If you want to trim a large laurel hedge by mechanical means, finish by trimming off any damaged areas with secateurs. Sliced leaves are not really a problem here, as they brown and drop off, and new growth fills the gaps.

GENERAL PRUNING RULES

Pruning should be timed to give the longest period for new growth to develop and harden off before the onset of winter. Most pruning should be done from late summer to early winter, or after flowering.

Hedgerows

Except for *Acer campestre*, hedgerow plants can be clipped very successfully with a good strong pair of hedge shears. *Acer campestre* really want to be medium-sized trees, so prune the strong growth back by one-third during the dormant winter months, using either strong secateurs or tree loppers: this encourages them to produce many more side shoots which will then become entwined with the neighbouring plants.

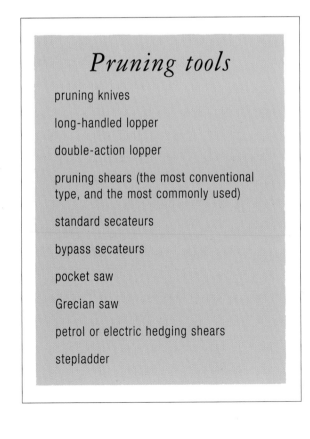

Pruning tools

pruning knives

long-handled lopper

double-action lopper

pruning shears (the most conventional type, and the most commonly used)

standard secateurs

bypass secateurs

pocket saw

Grecian saw

petrol or electric hedging shears

stepladder

Newly planted hedges

When first planted, prune back hard to encourage root growth. As a general rule, flowering hedges planted in autumn and winter should be reduced to between 6 and 9in (15 and 22cm) above the ground in early spring, before the growing season starts. This will encourage them to grow into thick, bushy plants. Evergreen plants, lilacs, broom and gorse should be trimmed lightly, with any untidy branches cut back.

However, if the hedge is planted in late spring, whether deciduous, flowering or evergreen, only a light trim is required the first year, leaving cutting back hard until the start of the following spring. Hedges planted later in the season need to retain as much foliage as possible in order to help them build up a strong root system: roots acquire much of their food through their leaves during the growing period. Cutting back hard in the late spring will cause the plant to suffer and very little progress will be made in the first season.

Ligustrum (privet), *Prunus spinosa* and *P. cerasifera* (myrobalan), tamarix and thorns should all be cut back hard in the winter and early spring while

Renewal pruning of a hornbeam hedge

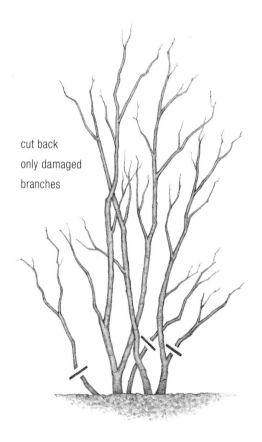

cut back
only damaged
branches

cut back all
branches

Cutting back hard

Cutting back lightly

deciduous hedges, such as hornbeam, beech and hazel, should be cut back by about one-third of their growth. The same principle applies to berberis, cotoneaster, laurels, lonicera and pyracantha. All other plants should be trimmed very lightly, leaving the leader shoot to grow away strongly.

Young hedges

Flowering shrubs

If no berry or fruiting interest occurs in the autumn or winter, prune back the flowering stems and clip into shape after flowering. If the shrub does produce berries or fruits, clip back after all the fruits have dropped off or been harvested, ie, in very late winter or early spring. Shrubs that produce flowers on the current season's growth, or on growth produced in the spring, should be pruned at the end of the winter, before the sap starts to rise. Shrubs that produce their flowers on the previous season's growth can be pruned as soon as the flowering period is over and the flowers have faded.

Evergreen hedges

These should be clipped and shaped in midsummer, as it is unlikely that they will put out much new growth later in the year. This timing allows the hedge to continue growing slowly and the new growth to harden off before the onset of winter. With evergreens it is important not to cut back into dead or very old wood as few evergreen plants, with the exception of yew, are responsive to such severe pruning. Evergreens invariably die back instead of rejuvenating when treated in this way, which means that new growth will not appear on the old wood. However, evergreen shrubs, such as lonicera, privet and box, do respond well to regular clipping throughout the growing season if you want to keep a formal shape tight.

Deciduous hedges

Deciduous trees and shrubs can be pruned at any time from midsummer to midwinter.

RENEWAL PRUNING

In a word, renewal pruning is revitalization. This should be done on a regular basis at the same time as cutting back the flowering or fruiting stems, or reducing the height or width of the hedge, in order to keep it vigorous and healthy.

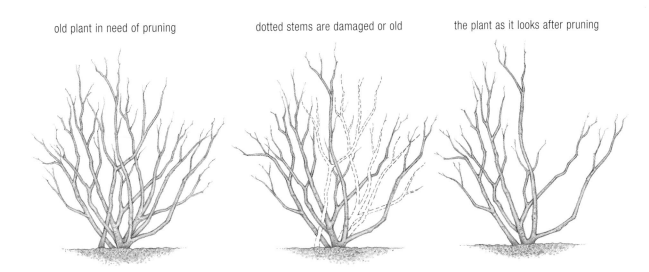

old plant in need of pruning   dotted stems are damaged or old   the plant as it looks after pruning

Renewal pruning

When not to prune

• Never prune after heavy rainfall: pruning necessitates tramping around the roots which compacts the soil, thus inhibiting its breathing and preventing the moisture from draining down to the roots. Wait until the ground is drier

• Never prune when it is frosty, snowing or icy winds are blowing

• Never prune when the plant's sap is rising – usually early spring. This will cause the plant to bleed and can lead to die-back

The oldest branches should be cut out annually to encourage fresh new growth from the base, particularly with flowering hedges as they produce a number of branches at ground level rather than one single trunk. Remove these branches after flowering unless fruits or berries are produced; in this case, remove them in early spring once the fruits are spent.

Established hedges

Once the hedge has settled down and the severe pruning – in order to establish a thick hedge – has been done, regular trimming is necessary to keep a hedge within bounds.

Hedges are living walls and boundaries and as such, they give both shape and style to a garden. It is essential that they are cared for properly in order to retain these features.

Shape

Theoretically, hedges should always be broader at the base and narrower at the top. This allows light to reach the lowest part of the hedge, allows rain to reach the soil around the roots of the hedge more easily, and also discourages the hedge from becoming top-heavy – this must not be allowed to happen. Formal hedges are particularly prone to this if they are not tapered from inception. Strong winds or a heavy snowfall on an already top-heavy hedge can have disastrous effects. The once upright wall of greenery could be blown apart or broken by nature's ravages. If the hedge is shaped correctly – wider at the bottom than the top – the chance of such disasters is more remote. Although the snow will still lie heavily on the hedge, the wider base

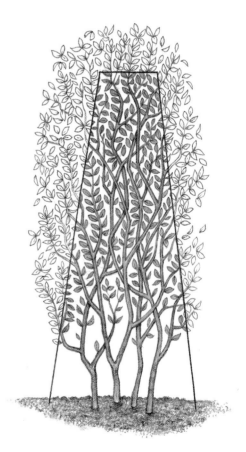

A hedge should always be pruned to keep a wedge shape

taut string

required height
of hedge

Pruning an established, formal hedge

will be able to support the weight. In practical terms then, the height of the hedge, particularly with formal hedges, should be sacrificed for a year or two whilst the base of the hedge thickens and strengthens.

Formal hedges

Formal hedges should generally be trimmed with mechanical or electrical shears or clippers. When pruning formal hedges it is quicker, and in the long run much more accurate, to stretch a piece of string at the height required, along the length of the hedge. Fix the string to an upright stake at either end of the hedge. With this in place, trim along the line of the string, always cutting to the lowest dip. If the hedge is growing against a fence or wall, use that as a guide either by following a particular line of bricks or a line on the fence panels.

The following diagrams explain how to trim a formal hedge from initial planting, in easy stages.

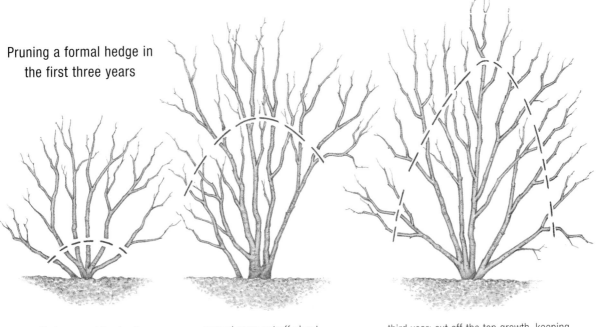

Pruning a formal hedge in
the first three years

first year: cut to about
6in (15cm) from ground

second year: cut off about
one-third of growth

third year: cut off the top growth, keeping
the hedge top narrower than the bottom

Once a year

For hedges that require pruning only once a year, including *Prunus laurocerasus* and *Elaeagnus* spp., late summer or early autumn is the best time. Late summer is an ideal time to trim any hedge if a yearly trim is all that can be managed. *Carpinus betulus* (hornbeam) and *Fagus sylvatica* (beech) will hold their drying leaves through most of the winter if pruned just the once in late summer.

The leaders – the most vigorous, tallest and upright shoots – should be trimmed only lightly, at the most by about one-third of their growth, until the required height is reached. Side shoots should be cut back fairly hard to stop the hedge from becoming too wide. Ideally, laurel and elaeagnus should be trimmed only once, in early autumn, but cut back fairly hard to keep a good shape.

Twice a year

For pruning twice a year the ideal times are midsummer and mid-autumn, to remove any new growth since the summer clipping. Included in this category are escallonias, conifers, holly and beech. Follow the pruning methods for the second and third years to ensure the development of a good, bushy hedge. In later years, always keep the leaders pruned hard and the sides of the hedge vertical or tapering.

To keep the hedge tapered, cut back the top growth by about one-third in the second year and cut the side shoots back hard, to within a few inches (around 7cm) of the start of the new growth. In the third year do the same again, but trim the leaders or upright shoots just lightly until the height required has been attained. Trim back hard every year when the hedge has reached the height you want but always keep the bottom of the hedge wider than the top.

Several times a year

Once established the faster-growing shrubs, such as *Crataegus monogyna*, ligustrum (privet), lonicera,

pinch off the dead flowers

Deadheading spent flowers

Prunus cerasifera and *Prunus spinosa* (blackthorn), should be trimmed several times a year. These shrubs grow quickly and need regular clipping. To encourage them to grow thickly at the base, cut down by half their size in their second year then cut back by a quarter of their height in subsequent years, until they are as high as you want. Always cut the side shoots back hard to encourage and maintain a thick hedge. Initially, this needs to be done in early or midsummer and then again in early or mid-autumn, but once the hedge is established and at the required height, clip several times a year to keep it looking crisp.

Informal flowering hedges

With informal, flowering hedges, always cut back cleanly above a bud and use a saw to cut back large branches or shoots, making sure no snags are left in the branches. However, more importantly, make sure you prune flowering hedges at the right time of year: if you get this wrong, you will lose a year's worth of flowers. Once established, pruning is only required once a year for informal hedging. Flowering, informal hedges are usually tidied with secateurs, by hand. Renewal pruning, taking out the old dead or diseased wood, and deadheading should be done at the same time.

Early flowering

This group covers shrubs which flower on the previous season's wood. These should be trimmed in summer after flowering. Prune selectively, as soon as the flowers have faded, by cutting back the flowering stems to new growth, as near the base as possible or to a dormant shoot as low as you can. This will encourage strong new growth at the base. The trimming should be done with secateurs or loppers. At the same time, cut out old, broken or dead wood. The hedge will look very thin at the time of pruning but will soon spring back into life, thicker than ever before and ready to produce flowers again for the next year.

Flowering twice a year

This group covers hedges which flower on the current season's wood. With a hedge producing flowers in summer and autumn, trim in early spring. All that needs to be done is to cut off the wood that produced the flowers the previous season and remove any dead or broken wood. This trimming is usually done in late winter or early spring. Cut back the old wood fairly hard so that the plants never get out of hand.

Flowering on spurs or side shoots

In this group are the rhododendrons and pyracanthas. This is the most straightforward of the groups: all that needs to be done is to cut back any long growths in early spring or autumn and deadhead the flowers. This stops the plant putting all its energy into producing seed heads. It is best to leave young plants to their own devices until they are fairly well established, then prune judiciously to allow them to thicken. Damaged or frosted branches and stems should be removed, along with spindly growth which is keeping light from the centre of the shrub.

NEGLECTED HEDGES

Neglected hedges are sometimes inherited when buying a property with an established garden. To grub up a hedge can be a costly and difficult business, and one to be resorted to only if no other course of action can be taken. The first step is to ascertain the hedge type in order to check what pruning it requires. Neglected hedges are often of the woody species, such as *Crataegus monongyna* (hawthorn), *Fagus sylvatica* (beech) or *Carpinus betulus* (hornbeam), which respond well to hard cutting back and ruthless thinning out.

They are also, invariably, full of dead wood and tangled, spindly branches and with a host of perennial weeds at their base. So, if you have decided to attempt a hedge restoration, the first job is to clean it up so that you can at least see its line and get some idea of its original shape and perhaps even its original height.

Leaving the height till last, try to thin out the hedge as much as possible by removing the perennial weeds and the dead and spindly wood. To begin, cut off any growths that are obviously at odds with the hedge shape. This alone will help invigorate the hedge by allowing light, air and water to reach the root system. It will also expose the areas in the hedge where large gaps have appeared and which may need filling in.

If the hedge is an evergreen or a shrub which will not tolerate really harsh treatment, such as holly, olearia, lavender and most of the conifers, you must thin it out with a lighter touch. Such plants will not respond to cutting back into their old wood and thinning out is the only way forward. Reduce the height to encourage stronger growth at the base.

Evergreen hedges should be tackled in the spring when the new growth is beginning. Winter is a good time for deciduous hedges, as the disturbance to wildlife will be minimal – it is also much easier to see exactly what you are doing and where you are cutting when the hedge is leafless.

An overgrown, mixed hedge in need of severe pruning

The same rules apply to the shaping of a neglected hedge as to a new or established one (see p 114). Pull a string tautly along the line of the hedge (see p 115) or lower a wooden 'A' frame over the hedge to give you a contour to clip to. Whilst feeding a regularly maintained, established hedge is not usually necessary, it does provide an additional stimulus for growth for a regenerated hedge.

A spring dressing of Growmore at 5oz per square yard (35g per square metre) will give an added boost. It is also important to conserve moisture while the hedge is getting back on its feet – a good mulch of garden or farmyard manure *after* rainfall will pay dividends (see p 120). It is worth taking all these measures before deciding to do away with an old hedge – you can still resort to this drastic action if your efforts are not rewarded.

Tools for pruning a neglected hedge

sharp, curved pruning saw

slasher or billhook (for perennial weeds)

pair of long-arm pruners (for the tall branches)

pair of stout secateurs (for the more accessible branches)

pair of good stout gloves

Care through the year

ABOVE The effects of wind scorching on *Euonymus japonicus*

NEWLY PLANTED HEDGES

If the hedge has been planted during late autumn or early winter, it is not difficult to keep the young root system moist – one of the most important factors – as autumn and winter rains will usually suffice. However, if it is planted from mid- to late spring, you should check regularly to make sure that the plants are getting plenty of water. Soak each plant thoroughly after planting, even to the point of virtually flooding them. Once the water has been absorbed into the ground, surround the base of the plants with a mulch of straw or peat to help conserve the moisture during drier periods. If it is quite late in the spring, grass cuttings can be used, but not too thickly as they generate heat. Lay the mulch over

Tools of the trade

wet soil so that it can hold in moisture if there is a dry spell. Shredded bark, grit, leaf mould and well-rotted garden compost can all be used. If the weather has been particularly inclement, check the young plants for frost or wind damage, and after high winds or gales, make sure they are still securely planted. If there are signs of frost or wind damage, carefully trim off any offending areas.

During the early months it is also important to hoe around the plants regularly to keep the soil loose and to discourage weeds. Weeds, nettles and couch grass in particular, should be removed as quickly as possible to stop them from taking over the soil and suffocating the new plants.

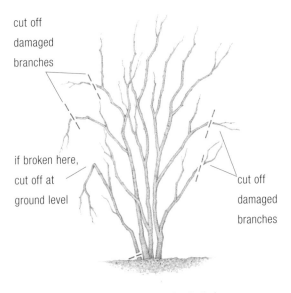

cut off damaged branches

if broken here, cut off at ground level

cut off damaged branches

Trimming off frost and wind damage

THROUGH THE YEAR

Hedges require a regular maintenance programme to run alongside your other garden chores. The monthly check list below sets out a good system. I have started in mid-autumn, when you should be buying new bare-root hedging plants and preparing to plant them out, whether you are rejuvenating an existing hedge or starting one from scratch.

Mid-autumn

This is the time to begin putting your garden to bed for the winter. Hedges need to be tidied up and the soil around them forked over. Weeds, dead leaves and any rubbish which may have collected around their stems should be gathered up and disposed of, along with the rest of the garden refuse – but take care not to disturb any hedgehogs. Any final trimming should be carried out now, and any dead or damaged branches should be removed and cut back to healthy wood. The planting of any type of hedge can be carried out at this time. Evergreens should be planted from early to mid-autumn as the soil will still be warm

enough to encourage new roots to form. Deciduous shrubs should always be planted when they are dormant, after the first frosts.

Late autumn

The planting of deciduous hedges can continue in late autumn and if it is warm enough, evergreens can still be planted out too. However, if the weather is very cold, evergreens will fare better planted in early spring. Neglected deciduous hedges can be cut back very hard at this time, while evergreens should be left until mid-spring before any drastic measures are taken. Even then, avoid cutting back into the old wood as die-back may occur.

Early winter

Early winter continues to see the planting of deciduous hedges so long as the ground is not frozen nor the weather too cold.

Midwinter

You can continue planting deciduous hedging if weather conditions permit. If you have bought bare-root plants and it is too cold to plant them out, make sure you keep their roots covered with straw or sacking and keep them in a frost-free place until the ground is soft enough for planting. Make sure the roots are wet before placing them in the sack and do not forget to keep the roots moist.

Keep a lookout for rabbit and mouse damage on newly planted hedges at this time of year: their bark is a very good source of winter food. Protect the bark with netting or, for the stems, special plastic, rabbit-proof covers which can be bought, very cheaply, at any good garden centre.

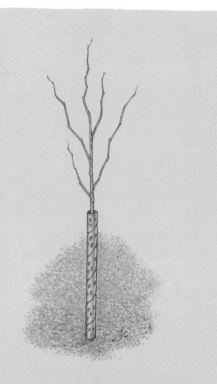

Protecting a young plant with a rabbit-proof cover

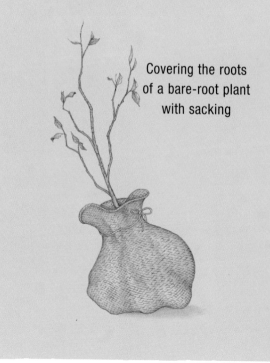

Covering the roots of a bare-root plant with sacking

Late winter

All planting of deciduous, flowering and formal hedging should now be finished. Check regularly for wind or gale damage to young plants. If you have bought pot-grown plants, now is the time to plant them out in your prepared areas. Established hedges should be fed at this time; spread top dressings around the base of the plants and fork them carefully into the ground. Well-rotted farmyard manure, good garden compost, and leaf mould are all good sources of nutrients. Growmore or Six-X chicken pellets, used sparingly, are also good slow-release fertilizers. Newly planted hedges, except the evergreens, should be cut back hard.

Early spring

Evergreens can be planted from the middle of early spring onwards and, in the milder areas, even at the very start of spring. Pot-grown shrubs can be planted out too. Continue top dressing and feeding and finish your pruning of all new hedging. Keep checking for wind damage and firm any young plants that have been disturbed back into the soil.

Mid-spring

Evergreens and pot-grown plants can still be planted at this time. Keep the soil around the newly planted hedges free from weeds. Evergreen shrubs can be trimmed back if necessary. Any of the early flowering hedges should be cut back as soon as the flowers fade, and the first trimming of newly planted hedges should be finished. If any of your hedges are infested with aphids or greenfly, this is the time to spray them, if you are not against using chemicals.

Late spring

Late spring sees the finish of the planting cycle as it is really only the last of the evergreens and any pot-grown plants that can be planted out at this time. Planting bare-rooted plants at the end of spring is always very risky: an unseasonably warm spell could see you spending all your time trying to keep the plants watered. Moisture is the key to getting a young hedge established as the plants all need plenty of water to get their root systems settled well into the ground. This is the time to cut back young hedging plants (those in their first year) hard so that their energy goes into producing strong roots rather than developing upper branches and leaves. A good, strong, bushy base is the key to a long-lived and attractive thick hedge. It is essential to keep weeds at bay during the fast-growing months so that the new plants do not get choked. Plants can be surrounded with a porous material, such as Mypex or shredded bark, which will suppress weeds but allow moisture to reach the soil beneath.

Early summer

Early summer requires only hoeing, mulching and watering around the new hedge plants; grass clippings will provide you with a good mulch but don't spread them thickly. Keep remembering to cut back the flowering hedge plants after the flowers fade and watch out for any pest damage. Cut out dead and damaged shoots and remove any plants that have not taken, remembering to replace them, if necessary, in mid-autumn.

Mid- and late summer

During mid- and late summer the tasks are the same as for early summer, with the addition of trimming formal hedges. Hedges of lavender, germander and santolina need cutting back hard after flowering to stop them from becoming leggy and woody but remember not to cut back into the old wood as this will damage the plant.

Early autumn

Early autumn and the cycle is nearly complete. Evergreens should be planted at this time for both formal and flowering hedging, and the tidying up process should be started once again.

Pests and diseases

HEDGE HEALTH

Many of the garden pests that attack roses, herbaceous plants and vegetable gardens also affect hedgerows. Hedges offer them a very cosy and protected environment but fortunately, most hedging plants are robust enough not to be badly affected by infestation or disease. Frost and wind probably do more damage to a hedge than any pests or diseases. Judicious pruning and general good husbandry – clearing out any rubbish and dead leaves in autumn and spring – go a long way to protecting a hedge. Watch out for hedgehogs when clearing a hedge: they are a favoured hibernation place, and the hedgehogs themselves feed on many garden pests.

However, pests and diseases can spoil the foliage and thus the overall appearance of a hedge if they are allowed to become established. The pests and diseases that most commonly affect hedging plants are listed below, along with the most effective measures of controlling them should they become a major problem. I have only touched on a huge subject here and do not profess to be an expert on the wide choice of insecticides and fungicides that are on the market. If you wish to increase your knowledge, *Collins' Guide to Pests, Diseases and Disorders of Garden Plants,* by Stefan Buczacki and Keith Harris, is packed with information.

LEFT Birch sawfly larvae

PESTS

Aphids

Aphids, including greenfly and blackfly, feed on the plant's sap, damaging the leaves and stems. They are most prevalent from early spring to mid-autumn (the growing season). Look out for the appearance of a sooty mould on the plant as this indicates their presence.

The most effective defence is to spray the plant with a chemical insecticide, and sometimes to apply a winter wash. Both systemic and non-systemic insecticides can be sprayed onto growing plants throughout the growing season.

Non-systemic sprays work through direct contact with the insects. They will curtail the aphids' activity without killing them, and will need to be reapplied if the infestation returns. However, if the problem is caught and treated early enough, they can be very effective.

Systemic insecticides are the more powerful, particularly where the aphids are protected by curled-up leaves or dense, bushy growth. These chemicals are absorbed into the plant's tissues, so the aphids ingest them along with the sap, no matter how well covered they are. A second spray will still be required if the infestation recurs.

Both types of insecticide can be bought from good garden centres, in aerosol cans for easy application. Non-systemic sprays are usually based on derris, malathion, pyrethrum and nicotine, while systemic sprays are based on diazinion, fenithrothion, primicarp and pirimiphos-methyl. These are the names you should look for when choosing an appropriate spray.

Winter washes, based on tar oil, can be used on deciduous, woody plants. They should be applied

Aphids feasting on sap

only when the plant is dormant. They can be sprayed or brushed onto the plant, and will kill any over-wintering aphid larvae. Evergreen plants should never be tar-washed, as the wash will scorch their leaves.

Caterpillars

The most common caterpillar to appear in your garden is that of the cabbage white butterfly. If these cause visible damage to the foliage of your hedge, you can use a general insecticide containing derris or malathion, or crush the larvae and caterpillars on a regular basis.

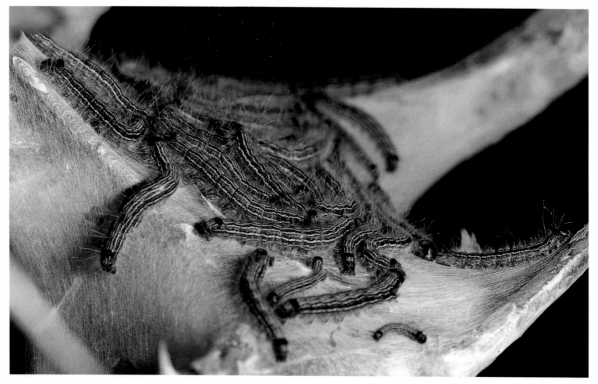

Lackey moth caterpillars on 'web'

Mealybugs and scale insects

Because of the proximity of hedging plants, infestations of these insects travel fast. If an infestation appears, deal with it as soon as possible. Use either a non-systemic insecticide containing malathion or nicotine, or a systemic insecticide containing formothion.

DISEASES

Moulds and mildews

These are generally only a problem in very humid weather and will be visible on affected leaves. Mildew can be dealt with by using chemical fungicide sprays. The most effective is zineb, a dithiocarbonate. Rust is best attacked by pruning out the damaged branches, the twigs and leaves of which will appear swollen and red or orange. It can also be treated with zineb.

Honey fungus

If you are very unlucky, one deadly disease that can attack a hedge is honey fungus. This will kill the roots of affected plants. The usual symptoms are wilt and die-back and the appearance of yellow-orange toadstools around the base of the plant. If you dig up the roots, you will find they are covered with very fine, thread-like white laces.

Once spotted, dig the plant up and burn it immediately or it will spread to the surrounding plants. This fungus cannot be treated with chemical sprays, and no other shrubs should be planted in its space for at least a year, to ensure that the fungus dies completely.

More often than not, honey fungus occurs in badly drained areas, so it is important that you facilitate good drainage when planting your hedge.

The distinctive yellow-orange toadstools of the honey fungus

SEASONAL TASKS TO HELP CONTROL PESTS AND DISEASES

Winter

Clear all rubbish and debris away from the base of the hedge, including dead leaves and wood. Apply a winter wash of tar oils to hedge plants that have been badly infested during the year to destroy over-wintering insects and their eggs. NB: use these washes – fungicides or insecticides – only on dormant woody, deciduous plants.

Early spring

Continue to clear out rubbish and debris from around the hedge, particularly if this has been overlooked during the winter months.

Mid-spring and the growing season

Spray both non-systemic and systemic insecticides to control aphids, mealybugs and scale insects as this is the season during which they are most prevalent. These sprays can be used on growing plants.

Late spring and summer

Continue to keep a look out for any infestation of pests and spray accordingly. If you don't like to use insecticides and you have the patience, remove caterpillars and their larvae from plants when you see them.

PICKINGS

A culinary bonus

Cooking with wild fruits and flowers

WILD FOOD

Most berries, crab apples and wild damsons are freely available in hedgerows in late summer and autumn. Always use wild fruits as soon as they are picked to reap the benefit of the flavours at their best. Many fruits and wild flowers can also be used medicinally and for making wine. If you are interested in these crafts, there are many books on countryside ingredients to guide you. The following is just a taste of the uses hedgerow fruits and flowers can be put to.

ABOVE Elderflower sprays
LEFT Elan apples

SLOE GIN

Distinctive festive liqueur

1 bottle of gin
1lb (450g) sloes
3oz (80g) sugar

Clean the sloes by rolling them in a clean cloth wrung out in boiling water. Prick each sloe twice with a sterilized needle and drop them into a large glass container. Add the sugar, seal the container, and shake every day for two weeks. Add a bottle of gin to this sloe and sugar mix and leave for three months in a cool place, giving the bottle an occasional shake. At the end of this time, drain off the liquid into a fresh bottle or wine decanter in two stages: first pour the contents through a strainer to separate the liquid from the sloes, then give the gin a final strain by pouring it through filter paper or a damp piece of muslin to remove any remaining sediment.

The strained sloes can be re-used by putting them in a punch bowl and adding a bottle of sparkling white wine. This makes a good aperitif for a Christmas Eve dinner.

SLOE AND APPLE JELLY

Delicious served with lamb or game

Equal weight of sloes and cooking apples
Water
Sugar as required

After wiping the sloes with a warm cloth and peeling the apples, place in a pan, add just enough water to cover and stew gently. Strain the fruit through a jelly bag and add 1lb (450g) sugar to each pint of juice recovered. Place the sugar and all the juice in a clean pan and stir until the sugar has completely dissolved. Bring to a rapid boil and leave boiling until a teaspoonful of the syrup sets on a cold saucer. If the mixture becomes tacky when cold and wrinkles when pushed with a finger, the setting point has been reached. Pour into small, hot jars, cover immediately with waxed paper circles and leave to cool. Once the jelly is cold, seal the jars with cloth or Cellophane covers.

CRAB APPLE JELLY

Ideal with game or pork dishes

Allow 1pt (600ml) water to every 1pt (600ml) of
    crab apples
Sugar as required

Place the water and apples in a pan. There is no
need to core or peel the apples, just wash
thoroughly and chop roughly. Simmer until the
fruit is a pulp. Pass this pulp through a muslin bag
and leave overnight to drip. Do not squeeze the
pulp from the bag as this will cloud the jelly.
Measure the liquid into a clean pan and allow 1lb
(450g) sugar to each pint (600ml). Stir gently over
a low heat until the sugar has completely dissolved,
then stir quickly until it reaches setting point. To
test for this, place a teaspoonful on a cold saucer. At
setting point this will become tacky when cold and
will wrinkle when pushed with a finger.

ELDERFLOWER VINEGAR

Good added to salad dressings

I have adapted the following two recipes from Gail
Duff's *The Countryside Cook Book*.

500ml bottle white wine vinegar
3oz (80g) elderflower sprays

Place the elderflowers in a large, screw-top jar
or bottle and add the vinegar. Leave on a sunny
window ledge for about a week. Strain off the
vinegar and pour it into a clean bottle.

HAWTHORN TEA

A lovely and refreshing drink

1 tbsp (15ml) hawthorn flowers
1 tbsp (15ml) lemon balm leaves
2 large sage leaves
1 large tsp (5ml) honey (more if you have
    a sweet tooth)

Chop all the flowers and leaves together and pour
1pt (600ml) of boiling water over them. Leave for
10–15 minutes, strain into a mug and sweeten
with honey to taste.

ROSEHIP TEA

A cleansing and invigorating drink

Several handfuls of rosehips (from any roses)
1pt (600ml) boiling water

Dry the rosehips in a dry, airy place, then crush them into very small pieces. The ideal way to do this is with a pestle and mortar. Take care here as the hips do stain. Store the crushed hips in a dark, airtight container. To make the tea, pour 1pt (600ml) of boiling water over 2tsp (10ml) of the crushed hips and infuse for 5–10 minutes to bring out the deep, rose pink colour.

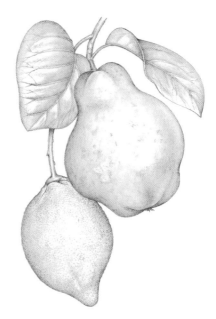

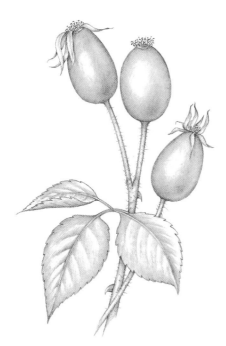

QUINCE JELLY

Great with cheese and biscuits

2lb (900g) quinces
3pts (1.8l) water
8tbsp (120ml) lemon juice and rind of 1 lemon
Granulated sugar, as required

Chop the washed quinces roughly and place them in a pan together with the water and lemon juice and the lemon rind tied in a muslin bag. Bring to the boil and leave to simmer for around 1½ hours, or until the fruit is tender. Remove the lemon rind then pour the quince pulp and cooking juice into a muslin-lined strainer and allow to drip through into a clean bowl. Do not squeeze or pummel the pulp. Measure the juice that has strained through and add 1lb (450g) sugar for each pint. Place the juice and sugar in a clean pan and bring to the boil, stirring until the sugar has dissolved. Continue boiling rapidly until the setting point has been reached.

To test for setting point, place a teaspoonful on a cold saucer; if a thin skin appears, the jelly is ready to bottle. Pour into hot, sterilized jars and cover.

NOMENCLATURE

*Understanding
botanical names*

Plant names

Plants are grouped, or classified, according to common characteristics. The names they are given indicate to which group they belong. The largest grouping, which is based on the structure of the plant's flowers, fruits and other organs, is the family. Families are then divided into genera and genera into species. Every plant has a botanical name which is composed of two parts, the first indicating its genus and the second its species. Sometimes, when referring generally to a number of species within a genus, the genus name will be used on its own, eg viburnum. To refer to a particular species, however, both names must be used, eg *Viburnum lantana, V. opulus.*

Species may be further divided into subspecies, which are groupings of plants within a species that share a particular characteristic or characteristics not found in the other plants within that species. A sub-species is indicated by the inclusion of 'subsp.' in the plant's name, eg *Aconitum napellus* subsp. *napellus.*

Additional names are allocated if the plant is a hybrid (a cross between different genera or species), a cultivar (a man-made variation; the result of a deliberate process of breeding), a variety (a naturally occurring variation as opposed to a man-made one) or a form (a plant with only a minor, but generally noticeable variation from the species, often in colour or size).

A hybrid plant is indicated by an 'x' in the plant's name, eg x *Cupressocyparis leylandii* (a genus hybrid), *Olearia* x *haastii* (a species hybrid).

The name of a cultivar is given within single quotes, eg x *Cupressocyparis leylandii* 'Galway Gold'. When it is clear what species is being referred to, a cultivar name may be given on its own, eg 'Aureum'. However, the same cultivar name may be used for many different plants belonging to different genera and species – *Viburnum lantana* 'Aureum' and *V. opulus* 'Aureum' are distinct plants, cultivars of different species within the same genera, and *Ribes alpinum* 'Aureum' is a cultivar belonging to a different genus. The genus acer includes three plants with the cultivar name 'Aureum'; *Acer cappadocium* 'Aureum', *A. palmatum* 'Aureum', and *A. shirasawanum* 'Aureum'.

A variety is indicated by 'var.', eg *Caltha palustris* var. *palustris*, and a form by 'f.', eg *Berberis thunbergii* f. *atropurpurea.*

Series or groups are collections of very similar hybrid cultivars of like parentage. They are easily identified by the word 'Series' or 'Group' in their name, eg *Viola* Ultima Series, *Aconitum napellus* subsp. *napellus* Anglicum Group.

Many plants are known by two names, or have been known by another name in the past; to avoid confusion, these names may be given as synonyms, eg *Rosa pimpinellifolia* (syn. *R. spinosissima*).

Common names (everyday names given outside the scientific system of nomenclature) are also used. The common name for buxus is box and that for acer is maple. These names may vary from country to country and even from region to region.

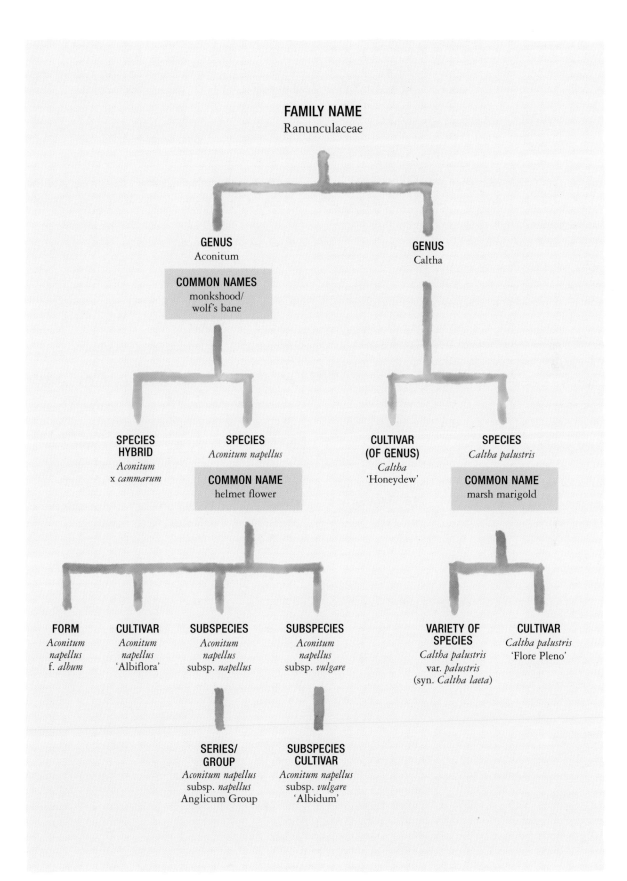

FAMILY NAME
Ranunculaceae

GENUS
Aconitum

COMMON NAMES
monkshood/
wolf's bane

GENUS
Caltha

**SPECIES
HYBRID**
*Aconitum
x cammarum*

SPECIES
Aconitum napellus

COMMON NAME
helmet flower

**CULTIVAR
(OF GENUS)**
Caltha
'Honeydew'

SPECIES
Caltha palustris

COMMON NAME
marsh marigold

FORM
*Aconitum
napellus
f. album*

CULTIVAR
*Aconitum
napellus*
'Albiflora'

SUBSPECIES
*Aconitum
napellus*
subsp. *napellus*

SUBSPECIES
*Aconitum
napellus*
subsp. *vulgare*

**VARIETY OF
SPECIES**
Caltha palustris
var. *palustris*
(syn. *Caltha laeta*)

CULTIVAR
Caltha palustris
'Flore Pleno'

**SERIES/
GROUP**
Aconitum napellus
subsp. *napellus*
Anglicum Group

**SUBSPECIES
CULTIVAR**
Aconitum napellus
subsp. *vulgare*
'Albidum'

Rose names

While roses follow the same system of naming as other plants, there are a few conventions peculiar to this genus. Firstly, they are classified into three main groups: species or wild roses, old garden roses, and modern garden roses. Species roses are naturally occurring species and species hybrids, while old and modern garden roses are cultivars.

Roses are also categorized by type, according to their growth and flowering habits. While these types have been reclassified by the World Federation of Rose Societies – in order to clarify overlapping categories – many growers and gardeners still use the old names and confusion reigns.

After 2,000 years of cultivation and breeding, there are many rose species that grow a little differently in the wild than in cultivation. When a rose has the tag 'hort.' next to its name, it is referring to the cultivated form. There are also many species that have more than one recognized name, past and present. As with any other species, these names may be given as synonyms.

Rose names may have two further peculiarities: colloquial names and trade names. Colloquial names are names that have not been registered, and are thus not officially recognized, but are nevertheless commonly used. Trade names are those that have been adopted for the purpose of selling a plant, because the official name is deemed unattractive in some way; it may be nonsensical, difficult to spell or remember, or simply not 'catchy'. A trade name is often translated or changed for selling in a different country, but the official name always remains the same.

MAIN TYPES OF ROSES

(old names still in common use appear in brackets)

alba	gallica	polyantha
Bourbon	ground cover	rambler
centifolia (Provence)	hybrid moss	rubiginosa hybrid
China	hybrid perpetual	rugosa
climbing	large-flowered (hybrid tea)	shrub
cluster-flowered (floribunda)	miniature	tea
damask	moss	
dwarf cluster-flowered (patio)	noisette	

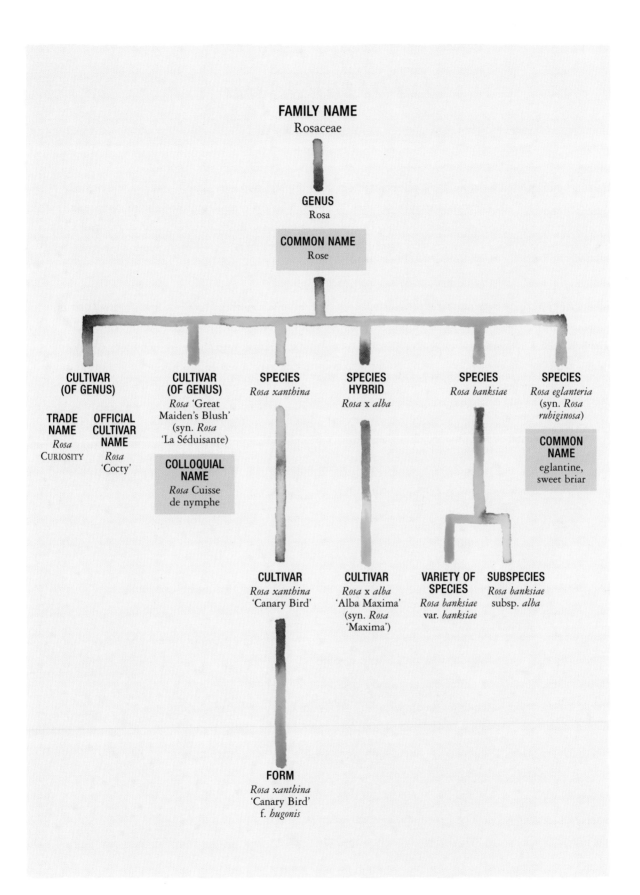

FAMILY NAME
Rosaceae

GENUS
Rosa

COMMON NAME
Rose

CULTIVAR (OF GENUS)

TRADE NAME
Rosa CURIOSITY

OFFICIAL CULTIVAR NAME
Rosa 'Cocty'

CULTIVAR (OF GENUS)
Rosa 'Great Maiden's Blush' (syn. *Rosa* 'La Séduisante)

COLLOQUIAL NAME
Rosa Cuisse de nymphe

SPECIES
Rosa xanthina

SPECIES HYBRID
Rosa x *alba*

SPECIES
Rosa banksiae

SPECIES
Rosa eglanteria (syn. *Rosa rubiginosa*)

COMMON NAME
eglantine, sweet briar

CULTIVAR
Rosa xanthina 'Canary Bird'

CULTIVAR
Rosa x *alba* 'Alba Maxima' (syn. *Rosa* 'Maxima')

VARIETY OF SPECIES
Rosa banksiae var. *banksiae*

SUBSPECIES
Rosa banksiae subsp. *alba*

FORM
Rosa xanthina 'Canary Bird' f. *hugonis*

Bibliography

Beales, Peter, *Twentieth-century Roses*, Harper & Row, New York, 1988

Buczacki, Stefan and Harris, Keith, *Pests, Diseases and Disorders of Garden Plants*, Collins, London, 1981

Cox, Peter and Kenneth, *Cox's Guide to Choosing Rhododendrons*, B. T. Batsford Ltd, London, 1992

Duff, Gail, *The Countryside Cook Book*, Prism Press, Dorset, 1982

Duff, Gail, *The Countryside Year Book*, Prism Press, Dorset, 1982

Dunnett, Nigel, 'At the Cutting Edge', *The Garden*, Vol 125 Pt 5, p 388, the Royal Horticultural Society

Fearnley-Whittingstall, Jane, *Ivies*, Chatto & Windus, London, 1992

Feltwell, Dr John, *A Guide to the Countryside*, Ward Lock Ltd, London, 1989

Glen, John 'Return to Camelot', *The Garden*, Vol 124 Pt 12, p 912, the Royal Horticultural Society

Hemphill, John and Rosemary, *The Fragrant Garden*, Bookmark Ltd, Enderby, 1991

Hillier Nurseries, *The Hillier Manual of Trees & Shrubs* (6th ed), David & Charles, Newton Abbot, 1991

Hobhouse, Penelope, *The Book of Gardening*, Frances Lincoln Ltd, London, 1994

Lancaster, Roy '*Sophora davidii*', *The Garden*, Vol 125 Pt 5, p 392, the Royal Horticultural Society

Latimer, Hugo, *The Mediterranean Gardener*, Frances Lincoln, London, 1990

Lawson-Hall, Toni and Rothera, Brian, *Hydrangeas: A Gardener's Guide*, Batsford Books, London, 1995

Le Rougetel, Hazel, *A Heritage of Roses*, Unwin Hyman Ltd, London, 1988

McVicar, Jekka, *Jekka's Complete Herb Book*, Kyle Cathie Ltd, London, 1994

Malins, Prof. John, *The Essential Pruning Companion*, David & Charles, Newton Abbot, 1992

Nicholson, B. E. and Gregory, S. A. M, *The Oxford Book of Wild Flowers*, Oxford University Press, Oxford, 1960

de Noailles, Vicomte and Lancaster, Roy, *Mediterranean Plants & Gardens*, Floraprint Ltd, Nottingham, 1990

Pollard, Hooper and Moore, *The Hedge*, Collins, London, 1974

Pollock, Michael, *Hedges & Screens*, Cassell Education, London, 1994

Rackman, Oliver, *The History of the Countryside*, J. M. Dent Ltd, London and Melbourne, 1986

Rose, Graham, *The Traditional Garden Book*, Dorling Kindersley, London, 1989

The Royal Horticultural Society Gardeners' Encyclopedia of Plants & Flowers (ed. Brickell, Christopher), Dorling Kindersley, London, 1989

Sackville-West, Vita, *The Garden Book*, Michael Joseph Ltd, London, 1986

Streeter, David and Richardson, Rosamund, *Discovering Hedgerows*, BBC, London, 1982

Thomas, Graham Stuart, *Shrub Roses of Today*, J. M. Dent & Sons Ltd, London, 1962

Whitehead, Jeffrey, *Hedges: How to Select, Plant & Grow*, Robert Hale, London, 1994

Glossary

bare-root plants, trees and shrubs in particular, which have been lifted out of the ground and delivered with little or no soil around their roots

canker this describes a disease which kills plant tissue, resulting in a lesion or wound. It is usually airborne and will strike indiscriminately

columnar growing in a narrow, slender form

conifer a tree or shrub with needle-like leaves and cone-like fruits, usually evergreen

container-grown plants which have been raised in pots or similar containers

cutting back pruning to rejuvenate or re-shape

deadhead to remove spent flower heads in order to encourage the production of more flowers

dormant in a period of suspended growth or rest

double digging to double dig is to dig trenches two spits of the spade deep and turn the soil into the trench in front but not mix the lower and upper spits of soil. This method is generally used for ground that has not been cultivated for a long time or to improve drainage

established settled on a permanent basis

fireblight a devastating bacterial plant disease. It kills the blossoms and leaves of shrubs and trees, turning them black/brown and making the plant look as though it has been scorched by fire

floriferous free-flowering

friable easily crumbled soil; can be raked to a tilth

habit a plant's characteristic growth, eg upright, spreading, or arching

hardy plants, trees and shrubs which can be grown outside all year round without any protection

heeling in to plant in a temporary position, in a trench or similar, until a permanent position has been chosen and prepared

loam a rich, easily worked mixture of soil, clay, sand and decayed vegetable matter

mulch a layer of organic material such as leaf-mould, straw, or decayed vegetable matter, which suppresses weeds and also feeds and helps to retain moisture around a plant. A mulch also helps maintain an even root temperature

parterre a flat, level area into which dwarf hedges are planted to enclose low-growing plants in an ornamental bed

potager a decorative vegetable garden

pruning the controlled cutting back of overgrown, dead or damaged parts in order to train, re-shape or promote new growth and flowering

renewal pruning the cutting out of all dead and damaged wood and cutting back of lateral shoots to encourage new, fresh growth

root ball the roots together with the soil or compost visible when a plant is removed from its container or dug up from the ground

specimen plant a striking plant, usually a tree or shrub, which is grown so that it can be viewed from all angles

shrub a woody plant which has many stems but no main central trunk

variegated leaves and stems having two or more contrasting markings

Index

About the author

Averil Bedrich has been a keen hands-on gardener for over 30 years. In that time she has created several gardens from scratch, including a sunken Elizabethan herb garden, rose and herbaceous beds and a water garden.

Her love of gardening began in the late 1960s. Neither she nor her husband, Gerry, come from gardening families, but with their cottage in north Buckinghamshire, they inherited an already established, if somewhat overgrown garden on about a quarter of an acre. With the help of some keen horticultural friends, and a steadily expanding collection of gardening books, their knowledge and enthusiasm increased and has never waned.

They have owned two nurseries, selling bare-root hedging plants and roses along with a vast selection of unusual herbaceous plants and shrubs, mail-order. This developed into a virtual correspondence school, with Averil and Gerry giving advice on designing, planting and maintaining hedges over the telephone.

From her home, now in East Sussex, Averil has been able to visit many of the famous gardens in the south of England, a source of inspiration for ideas on formal and informal flowering hedges. Her frequent trips to the South of France, where she has a second home, encouraged her to write a number of articles on tender plants and increased her knowledge of interesting climbers and unusual hedging.

She has written for *Period House and its Garden* and has contributed several articles to both *Garden Calendar* and *Exotic and Greenhouse Gardening*.

TITLES AVAILABLE FROM
GMC Publications

BOOKS

WOODCARVING

The Art of the Woodcarver	*GMC Publications*
Beginning Woodcarving	*GMC Publications*
Carving Architectural Detail in Wood:	
The Classical Tradition	*Frederick Wilbur*
Carving Birds & Beasts	*GMC Publications*
Carving the Human Figure: Studies in Wood and Stone	*Dick Onians*
Carving Nature: Wildlife Studies in Wood	*Frank Fox-Wilson*
Carving Realistic Birds	*David Tippey*
Decorative Woodcarving	*Jeremy Williams*
Elements of Woodcarving	*Chris Pye*
Essential Woodcarving Techniques	*Dick Onians*
Lettercarving in Wood: A Practical Course	*Chris Pye*
Making & Using Working Drawings	
for Realistic Model Animals	*Basil F. Fordham*
Power Tools for Woodcarving	*David Tippey*
Relief Carving in Wood: A Practical Introduction	*Chris Pye*
Understanding Woodcarving	*GMC Publications*
Understanding Woodcarving in the Round	*GMC Publications*
Useful Techniques for Woodcarvers	*GMC Publications*
Wildfowl Carving – Volume 1	*Jim Pearce*
Wildfowl Carving – Volume 2	*Jim Pearce*
Woodcarving: A Complete Course	*Ron Butterfield*
Woodcarving: A Foundation Course	*Zoë Gertner*
Woodcarving for Beginners	*GMC Publications*
Woodcarving Tools & Equipment Test Reports	*GMC Publications*
Woodcarving Tools, Materials & Equipment	*Chris Pye*

WOODTURNING

Adventures in Woodturning	*David Springett*
Bert Marsh: Woodturner	*Bert Marsh*
Bowl Turning Techniques Masterclass	*Tony Boase*
Colouring Techniques for Woodturners	*Jan Sanders*
Contemporary Turned Wood:	*Ray Leier, Jan Peters,*
New Perspectives in a Rich Tradition	*& Kevin Wallace*
The Craftsman Woodturner	*Peter Child*
Decorating Turned Wood: The Maker's Eye	*Liz & Michael O'Donnell*
Decorative Techniques for Woodturners	*Hilary Bowen*
Fun at the Lathe	*R.C. Bell*

Illustrated Woodturning Techniques	*John Hunnex*
Intermediate Woodturning Projects	*GMC Publications*
Keith Rowley's Woodturning Projects	*Keith Rowley*
Making Screw Threads in Wood	*Fred Holder*
Turned Boxes: 50 Designs	*Chris Stott*
Turning Green Wood	*Michael O'Donnell*
Turning Miniatures in Wood	*John Sainsbury*
Turning Pens and Pencils	*Kip Christensen & Rex Burningham*
Understanding Woodturning	*Ann & Bob Phillips*
Useful Techniques for Woodturners	*GMC Publications*
Useful Woodturning Projects	*GMC Publications*
Woodturning: Bowls, Platters, Hollow Forms, Vases,	
Vessels, Bottles, Flasks, Tankards, Plates	*GMC Publications*
Woodturning: A Foundation Course (New Edition)	*Keith Rowley*
Woodturning: A Fresh Approach	*Robert Chapman*
Woodturning: An Individual Approach	*Dave Regester*
Woodturning: A Source Book of Shapes	*John Hunnex*
Woodturning Jewellery	*Hilary Bowen*
Woodturning Masterclass	*Tony Boase*
Woodturning Techniques	*GMC Publications*
Woodturning Tools & Equipment Test Reports	*GMC Publications*
Woodturning Wizardry	*David Springett*

WOODWORKING

Advanced Scrollsaw Projects	*GMC Publications*
Beginning Picture Marquetry	*Lawrence Threadgold*
Bird Boxes and Feeders for the Garden	*Dave Mackenzie*
Complete Woodfinishing	*Ian Hosker*
David Charlesworth's Furniture-Making	
Techniques	*David Charlesworth*
David Charlesworth's Furniture-Making	
Techniques – Volume 2	*David Charlesworth*
The Encyclopedia of Joint Making	*Terrie Noll*
Furniture-Making Projects for the Wood Craftsman	*GMC Publications*
Furniture-Making Techniques for	
the Wood Craftsman	*GMC Publications*
Furniture Projects	*Rod Wales*
Furniture Restoration (Practical Crafts)	*Kevin Jan Bonner*
Furniture Restoration: A Professional at Work	*John Lloyd*

Furniture Restoration and Repair for Beginners — *Kevin Jan Bonner*
Furniture Restoration Workshop — *Kevin Jan Bonner*
Green Woodwork — *Mike Abbott*
The History of Furniture — *Michael Huntley*
Intarsia: 30 Patterns for the Scrollsaw — *John Everett*
Kevin Ley's Furniture Projects — *Kevin Ley*
Making & Modifying Woodworking Tools — *Jim Kingshott*
Making Chairs and Tables — *GMC Publications*
Making Chairs and Tables – Volume 2 — *GMC Publications*
Making Classic English Furniture — *Paul Richardson*
Making Heirloom Boxes — *Peter Lloyd*
Making Little Boxes from Wood — *John Bennett*
Making Screw Threads in Wood — *Fred Holder*
Making Shaker Furniture — *Barry Jackson*
Making Woodwork Aids and Devices — *Robert Wearing*
Mastering the Router — *Ron Fox*
Minidrill: Fifteen Projects — *John Everett*
Pine Furniture Projects for the Home — *Dave Mackenzie*
Practical Scrollsaw Patterns — *John Everett*
Router Magic: Jigs, Fixtures and Tricks to
  Unleash your Router's Full Potential — *Bill Hylton*
Router Tips & Techniques — *GMC Publications*
Routing: A Workshop Handbook — *Anthony Bailey*
Routing for Beginners — *Anthony Bailey*
The Scrollsaw: Twenty Projects — *John Everett*
Sharpening: The Complete Guide — *Jim Kingshott*
Sharpening Pocket Reference Book — *Jim Kingshott*
Simple Scrollsaw Projects — *GMC Publications*
Space-Saving Furniture Projects — *Dave Mackenzie*
Stickmaking: A Complete Course — *Andrew Jones & Clive George*
Stickmaking Handbook — *Andrew Jones & Clive George*
Storage Projects for the Router — *GMC Publications*
Test Reports: *The Router* and
  Furniture & Cabinetmaking — *GMC Publications*
Veneering: A Complete Course — *Ian Hosker*
Veneering Handbook — *Ian Hosker*
Woodfinishing Handbook (Practical Crafts) — *Ian Hosker*
Woodworking with the Router: Professional
  Router Techniques any Woodworker can Use — *Bill Hylton
  & Fred Matlack*
The Workshop — *Jim Kingshott*

UPHOLSTERY

The Upholsterer's Pocket Reference Book — *David James*
Upholstery: A Complete Course (Revised Edition) — *David James*
Upholstery Restoration — *David James*
Upholstery Techniques & Projects — *David James*
Upholstery Tips and Hints — *David James*

TOYMAKING

Restoring Rocking Horses — *Clive Green & Anthony Dew*
Scrollsaw Toy Projects — *Ivor Carlyle*
Scrollsaw Toys for All Ages — *Ivor Carlyle*

DOLLS' HOUSES AND MINIATURES

1/12 Scale Character Figures for the Dolls' House — *James Carrington*
Architecture for Dolls' Houses — *Joyce Percival*
The Authentic Georgian Dolls' House — *Brian Long*
A Beginners' Guide to the Dolls' House Hobby — *Jean Nisbett*
Celtic, Medieval and Tudor Wall Hangings in
  1/12 Scale Needlepoint — *Sandra Whitehead*
The Complete Dolls' House Book — *Jean Nisbett*
The Dolls' House 1/24 Scale: A Complete Introduction — *Jean Nisbett*
Dolls' House Accessories, Fixtures and Fittings — *Andrea Barham*
Dolls' House Bathrooms: Lots of Little Loos — *Patricia King*
Dolls' House Makeovers — *Jean Nisbett*
Dolls' House Window Treatments — *Eve Harwood*
Easy to Make Dolls' House Accessories — *Andrea Barham*
Heraldic Miniature Knights — *Peter Greenhill*
How to Make Your Dolls' House Special:
  Fresh Ideas for Decorating — *Beryl Armstrong*
Make Your Own Dolls' House Furniture — *Maurice Harper*
Making Dolls' House Furniture — *Patricia King*
Making Georgian Dolls' Houses — *Derek Rowbottom*
Making Miniature Food and Market Stalls — *Angie Scarr*
Making Miniature Gardens — *Freida Gray*
Making Miniature Oriental Rugs & Carpets — *Meik & Ian McNaughton*
Making Period Dolls' House Accessories — *Andrea Barham*
Making Tudor Dolls' Houses — *Derek Rowbottom*
Making Victorian Dolls' House Furniture — *Patricia King*
Miniature Bobbin Lace — *Roz Snowden*
Miniature Embroidery for the Georgian Dolls' House — *Pamela Warner*
Miniature Embroidery for the Tudor
  and Stuart Dolls' House — *Pamela Warner*
Miniature Embroidery for the Victorian Dolls' House — *Pamela Warner*
Miniature Needlepoint Carpets — *Janet Granger*
More Miniature Oriental Rugs & Carpets — *Meik & Ian McNaughton*
Needlepoint 1/12 Scale: Design Collections
  for the Dolls' House — *Felicity Price*
New Ideas for Miniature Bobbin Lace — *Roz Snowden*
The Secrets of the Dolls' House Makers — *Jean Nisbett*

CRAFTS

American Patchwork Designs in Needlepoint — *Melanie Tacon*
A Beginners' Guide to Rubber Stamping — *Brenda Hunt*
Beginning Picture Marquetry — *Lawrence Threadgold*

GARDENING

PHOTOGRAPHY

VIDEOS

Drop-in and Pinstuffed Seats	*David James*	Twists and Advanced Turning	*Dennis White*
Stuffover Upholstery	*David James*	Sharpening the Professional Way	*Jim Kingshott*
Elliptical Turning	*David Springett*	Sharpening Turning & Carving Tools	*Jim Kingshott*
Woodturning Wizardry	*David Springett*	Bowl Turning	*John Jordan*
Turning Between Centres: The Basics	*Dennis White*	Hollow Turning	*John Jordan*
Turning Bowls	*Dennis White*	Woodturning: A Foundation Course	*Keith Rowley*
Boxes, Goblets and Screw Threads	*Dennis White*	Carving a Figure: The Female Form	*Ray Gonzalez*
Novelties and Projects	*Dennis White*	The Router: A Beginner's Guide	*Alan Goodsell*
Classic Profiles	*Dennis White*	The Scroll Saw: A Beginner's Guide	*John Burke*

MAGAZINES

WOODTURNING • WOODCARVING • FURNITURE & CABINETMAKING

THE ROUTER • WOODWORKING

THE DOLLS' HOUSE MAGAZINE • WATER GARDENING

OUTDOOR PHOTOGRAPHY • BLACK & WHITE PHOTOGRAPHY

BUSINESSMATTERS

The above represents a full list of all titles currently published or scheduled to be published.
All are available direct from the Publishers or through bookshops, newsagents and specialist retailers.
To place an order, or to obtain a complete catalogue, contact:

GMC PUBLICATIONS

Castle Place 166 High Street Lewes East Sussex BN7 1XU United Kingdom
Tel: 01273 488005   Fax: 01273 478606
E-mail: pubs@thegmcgroup.com

Orders by credit card are accepted